In Troy Wake

Amanda Legault

IN MY WAKE
Copyright © 2016 by Amanda Legault

Printed in Canada

ISBN: 978-1-4866-1188-1

Word Alive Press
131 Cordite Road, Winnipeg, MB R3W 1S1
www.wordalivepress.ca

Library and Archives Canada Cataloguing in Publication

Legault, Amanda, 1987-, author
   In my wake / Amanda Legault.

Issued in print and electronic formats.
ISBN 978-1-4866-1188-1 (paperback).--ISBN 978-1-4866-1189-8 (pdf).--
ISBN 978-1-4866-1190-4 (html).--ISBN 978-1-4866-1191-1 (epub)

   1. Legault, Amanda, 1987-. 2. Coma patients--Biography.
3. Cognition disorders--Patients--Biography. 4. Traffic accident victims--Biography. I. Title.

RB150.C6L44 2015   616.8'49   C2015-907235-2
                                       C2015-907236-0

To my Heavenly Father, who loved me relentlessly
even while I broke His heart relentlessly. I love You.

To my husband, Kyle, who kept our wedding vows
even before they were spoken. I love you.

Contents

Foreword

I am Amanda's pastor. This morning, Amanda asked me to make good on a promise. In the early stages of Amanda's accident recovery, I told her that someday, she would write a book, and when completed I would write the foreword to it. What a privilege to introduce her God Story.

Two weeks after Amanda rededicated her life to make Jesus Christ both her saviour and Lord, Amanda faced the beginnings of what will likely be the greatest test of her life. Amanda's SUV broadsided a semi-trailer at near speed limit, and was dragged sideways under the belly of the trailer. It reduced her Durango to an oversized go-cart. Though it took only seconds, this would alter many lives—some for all of eternity.

The Bible says, *"God is our refuge and strength, an ever-present help in trouble. Therefore we will not fear... "* (Psalm 46:1–2). They say that perspective changes the view; in every storm, we get to choose to focus on God or focus on the trouble. Our fear diminishes as we fix our eyes on the God who is our refuge and strength.

But this is easier said than done. There are times in the centre of trouble when God simultaneously seems to be both distant and yet the only one we have to hold on to. When we wait for His miraculous hand to bail us out of trouble, and fail to see movement, God seems distant, yet His presence is amazing. His peace gives us comfort beyond comprehension in the midst of storms. God can seem so close that you can feel like His arms are holding you.

Amanda's boyfriend and family experienced this rollercoaster of emotions in the early part of the storm while Amanda was in a coma. Later, Amanda would feel the same emotions, amplified many times over, as she waited for the pain to go away and her abilities to return.

Tragedy always leaves a string of victims in its wake. I will never forget where I was when I got the call. Neither will Amanda's boyfriend Kyle, family members, or the members of the volunteer firefighters who spent hours with the Jaws of Life rescuing their small hometown gal. What you will read in the pages ahead is nothing less than the account of a modern-day miracle, written from an "inside-out" perspective.

My first glimpse of Amanda was in the ICU unit as I joined her mother to pray over her daughter. The gowned surgical team was waiting to take Amanda to the OR for surgery. She looked lifeless, like a pincushion with more tubes and wires than I had ever seen come from one body. Hope seemed unrecognizable—too distant to distinguish with natural eyes.

The Bible records that Ezekiel once saw God raise dead bones back to life. Although Amanda wasn't clinically dead, this is how those closest to Amanda felt; in slow motion, we would see a miracle unfold, as prayer and God's hand moved in tandem.

Waiting room family dynamics speak the cries of the soul during the storm of trauma: a father so badly hurting for his daughter that his words are few, his restlessness swelling from the frustration of not being able to fix her; a mother of faith continually calls the family to prayer for healing, and a spirit of wisdom and revelation for the medical staff; brothers and sisters intercede in prayer and support each other; an unbelieving boyfriend becomes a believer through a simple but foolish prayer ("God, if you are real, give me Amanda's pain"). God proved His reality by instantly answering this prayer with an excruciating three-day neck ache. A sinner's prayer then changed Kyle for all eternity. Through the entire journey, he demonstrated the love and faithfulness of a seasoned veteran.

In the beginning, the predominant rhythm seemed to be two steps back, one step forward. Amanda seemed to flirt with death, but tomorrow would always be another day with fresh hope. Many prayers were spoken as the trouble raged on. Then hope shimmered through like the first rays of morning light. Amanda was upgraded to an ICU stepdown unit.

About three weeks after the accident, Amanda spoke her first words. After forty-five minutes of speaking God's Word of healing and miracles from the Gospels, and speaking Psalm 103:1–5 repeatedly to an unresponsive

Amanda, a faint whisper slipped through her lips: "Jesus... Jesus... love Jesus... love Jesus... love Jesus."

Family and friends saw the miracle unfold, yet these steps were only the beginnings of Amanda's most difficult journey. After coming out of her coma, she experienced the full impact of her trouble: excruciating pain from a broken neck, having to learn to swallow and speak and walk again, and enduring the heartbreak of watching her impatient toddler unwilling to sit still enough so she could touch her with a mother's love. Through prayer, pain, and perseverance, we jointly witnessed the miracle of "dead bones" coming to life.

This book will give you a glimpse of the miracle from another perspective. You will see the miracle of God restoring dead bones from the inside out as Amanda tells the story of God restoring her life with the blessing of healing. While still bearing some reminders of the past, she now lives a new normal. Amanda reveals an incredible journey that will inspire hope from that inside-out perspective.

If you, a family member, or friend need to see hope in a world of darkness and despair, Amanda's story will be a breath of fresh air. Her story is real—its disjointed beginnings reflect the blank spots in her memory, to increasing clarity of the lows and highs, frustrations and celebrations, of a long, hard road to recovery. Amanda's faith to face the future comes through hearing the truth of God's Word and the testimonies of His works. You will be inspired to hope when hope feels distant, encouraged to persist when quitting wells up inside you, and even come to understand the schizophrenic rhythm of the Psalms. You will be drawn to Amanda's healer and God. Hope will rise as you see that miracles still happen!

This book is a must-read for those working in rehabilitation facilities or those who have family or close friends going through trauma. It will give you a perspective that can only be imagined. It will demonstrate your value and need for sensitivity as you stand with those in deep pain, and encourage you to remain faithful to your assigned task.

Be blessed as Amanda shares her heart and her God Story. Draw from the experiences of her wake to waken hope for your own journey.

—Pastor Glen Siemens

Oblivion

I'm driving along the 201, thoughts of Kyle strumming my mind.

I can't deal with him. How is this going to work? He doesn't—

A blaring horn wrenches me out of my reverie. I focus on the road ahead, and what seems like just inches in front of my Durango is an intersection with a semi barrelling through it.

I blink hard.

Still there.

I slam on the brakes, rip my hands off the wheel, and throw my arms over my head—

Black

White

Faces

Wordless

voices

Bailey

Bailey

Bailey...

Beep

beep

beep

Convulsions
of

agony   hold

me in

a

vice
grip

Beep

beep

beep

Beep

beep
beep

Weeping

Hands
on   my

arms

Why   are you
crying?

Beep

beep

beep

Beep   beep

    beep

                              Echoes
                              of grief

          Why
    are you crying?

                    Beep   beep

                    beep

Beep   beep

beep

"Traumatic brain injury…"
"…comminuted fracture C1, compression fracture C6…"

Who are you?
Are you talking to me?

"…hemothorax contusion…"
"…diffuse axonal injury… haemorrhages… left lobe collapse…"

What are you saying?

Beep   beep   beep

Beep   beep   beep

"I love you, Amanda."
Who is Amanda? Who is talking?

Black

I blink—try to blink—my eyes won't open
"Who are you?" I ask

Mouth doesn't move

"Listen to me," I demand
Mouth doesn't move

"I'm here!" I scream

Mouth doesn't move

White pinhole

Flames beneath my eyes
                              Beneath my eyes?
                    Where are my eyes?

The thought of blinking the fire away drifts around—how do I blink?

Tremors somewhere
Torment

"She's moving! Her eyelids are twitching! Her hand!"
What?

Black

Torture

A hairline of blinding whiteness attacks me
                    —my eyes, it stabs my eyes.

Ecstasy at finding my eyes. I squeeze my eyelids.

        Whiteness vanishes.
Oh!
    I force my eyelids apart.
        Whiteness transforms into a blurred mass of every colour.

    Pain, such pain.
    My eyes snap shut.

"Amanda! Oh baby girl, Amanda!"

        Who is Amanda?

A tornado assaults the cloud of my consciousness, all of me in senseless agony.

A trembling hand grasps mine.

My hand! I know my hand!

Electricity runs through me with thoughts to grip this hand. Why would I do that? *How* would I do that? My entire arm jerks.

Arm? My arm!

"Oh Amanda, I know you're trying to squeeze my hand. I know. I'm here! You're going to be fine, do you hear me?"

Who are you? Are you talking to me?

"Amanda, come back to us. Bailey is waiting for you. Kyle is waiting for you."

Bailey! I know that word … name! I know that name!

A low sound painfully pushes out of my throat. I know a baby girl, Bailey. I know her!

"Oh Amanda!" this woman with me proclaims with a quivering voice. "Can you open your eyes if you know Bailey?"

I know Bailey. I know Amanda. I know that I know them, but who are they to me? Who are they?

So cautiously, so hopefully, someone takes the side of my face in their hand. The woman urges me again.

"Amanda, can you open your eyes? Can you squeeze my hand?" A hand falls into mine again. "Can you show me you hear me?" Such hope, yet such uncertainty.

There is no new exclamation of joy from this woman. That means Amanda is not responding.

Oh! Amanda?

I don't know who I am. I know Amanda's name. I don't know who Amanda is.

Am I Amanda?

I focus all my meagre perception on my eyes. I know where my eyes are.

They fly wide open. Again, blurred mass of what, I cannot tell. I widen my eyes.

"Amanda, oh Amanda." This woman's yelps pierce my temples, my eyes, the fire beneath the surface.

Exhaustion swallows me. I close my unblinking, scorching eyes.

I am Amanda.

"Bailey, here's Mommy! Here's your Mommy."

A blur of something other than black.

"She opened her eyes when she heard Bailey! Nurse!"

"Mama? Mama night-night."

I know that sweet voice. I know Bailey.

Too much. I don't know why. My eyes and my face are burning.

I close my eyes.

"Can I put you beside Mommy?"

Giggles.

Do that again.

Small, warm body beside me. Tiny hands lay on top of the fire.

"Mama all done sleep."

Oh, Bailey, I know you.

The fire gets hotter. A wet drop escapes it.

"Oh Bailey, your mommy knows you! Mommy has tears for you, baby girl. She loves you so much."

Baby girl. Bailey.

Whispers of memories.

Oblivion.

"We can't do a whole lot for her mental capacity. Now it's up to her. She is strong. She has kept her heart beating through all of this, and that makes it clear that Amanda has a chance to pull through this and be okay."

"Please don't lose hope. We will admit her to Riverview, which is a first-rate rehabilitation hospital. Amanda is very fortunate. They have quite the waiting list, but with her circumstances, they'll have room for her on May 14. There, she'll have the best tools and the best chance to come as far as she can."

"She's only twenty one-and she has Bailey! She will be okay, she's strong. I know my girl will be okay…"

"I'm fine," I say without moving my mouth. Cursed mouth.

I open my eyes.

Blackness.

I blink. My eyes aren't open.

"Hello, Amanda, I'm Dr. Johnson. How are you today?" asks a blurry shadow that looks like the other phantoms that have come in and out of my room.

My eyes bore holes into her scrubs as I consider her words.

I'm so tired. My head is on fire. I close my eyes in a useless attempt to drown the furnace.

"Amanda, can you look at me?"

I open my eyes and glance in the direction of the voice. An obscure form stands over me and takes my hand in her latex-covered one. She uses a gloved finger to wet my papery lips with a bead of water.

I pour every trace of strength into the slow, labored blinks of my eyelids. I need to put out the flames in my head.

They're not just in my head. Fire is everywhere.

"Uuugh," I rasp, moving my hand sluggishly toward my throat. It lands on cold, hard plastic.

"Yes, my dear, we'll get you to drink this. I know it hurts." The woman moves her hand away and my bed sits me halfway up.

What is going on? Why is there an inferno in every ounce of my body? Who is this woman? Where am I?

"Amanda, after I give you some instructions, you're going to take a tiny sip," Shadow Woman says.

Gently, she puts a cup against my bottom lip and tilts it just enough for a glorious drop of thick liquid to almost contact my parched mouth. I start to open my mouth in response. My chin collides with something and my jaw painfully locks. The reprieve of liquid forgotten, I move my hand toward the unbending plastic pressing on my throat, desperately seeking an edge to pull it off.

Shadow Woman encloses my hand firmly in her own and puts it beside me. "Amanda, you need to leave your CTO alone." She stresses each word fiercely. "Your neck is broken. This neck brace absolutely has to be on you. Do not pull on it. Please, do not pull on it."

Broken neck. Broken neck?

As I vaguely ponder her words and actions, concrete weariness strikes every part of me. My heavy eyelids fall.

"Amanda, can you please listen to what I'm going to say? You need to understand how to do this safely," the doctor says as she lightly squeezes my hand. My eyelids peel apart. She raises the cup to my lips. "Now, hold your breath. Then when the fluid is on your tongue, press it against the roof of your mouth and squeeze your throat muscles together. Immediately after, clear you throat, okay?"

She waits for me to look in the direction of her face before tilting the cup. Jellylike fluid greets my sandpaper tongue.

"Hold your breath while you swallow, Amanda." Dr. Shadow quickly pulls back the cup. My mind is at war with this tiny drop of lifeblood. How do I swallow? "Press your tongue against the top of your mouth, squeeze your throat muscles together, and remember, do not take a breath while you do that."

After a long pause, I hold my breath and follow her instructions.

This lifeblood is gasoline to the fire. An explosion of blades rocks my neck, skull, and back as I gasp and squeeze my eyes shut. Shadow Woman slips one hand beneath the insane, rigid choke hold on my neck, and the other on top of my shoulder. She gently moves my head down onto my pillow.

"That was a good try, but you must not lift your head. Especially not so fast. I know you need a drink, but relax your head. You spine is fractured, Amanda."

What little I can make of the blur in front of me begins to spin as I attempt to understand what she's said. Spine fractured? What does that mean? That means I'm dead. This really is a dream.

Obviously people die when they break their spine or neck or whatever this lady is telling me. Don't they?

The thick fog of hell condenses around me. Sleep beckons me powerfully as I sink deeper into my nightmare.

I groggily try to turn over but am stopped by a sharp, paralyzing pain shooting through my neck, followed by the ludicrous realization that I'm wearing some kind of extremely tight collar. Alarmed, I move to sit up but am stopped again by senseless pain and a strap across my bed's side rails. This sets off some kind of buzzing.

A person—maybe two people—enters the room.

"What is this?" My voice comes out in a scratchy half-whisper.

"You're at Riverview Health Centre in Winnipeg, Manitoba," a man says in a calm, matter-of-fact voice. "I'm Tom, the nurse on this shift. You were in a car accident on April 22 that broke your neck, and the neck brace is there to set your spine as it heals. The restraints on your bed are to tell us when you're trying to get up, so we can help you. You can't walk right now."

I stare through squinted eyes at this blurred, alien man, waiting to recognize anything about his distorted image.

"Now dear, dinner will be served in about ten minutes, and Kyle and your mom should be here shortly. Let me just get you cleaned up here first."

This overload of inconceivable information stuns me. I'm obviously dreaming.

Tom moves closer to remove my blankets and lift my hospital gown. He pulls on something at my hip that sounds like a diaper being opened.

My disbelief is too great to respond in any way. I don't move a muscle, just allow Tom to handle my body in any way he has to in order to do what he's doing, which appears to be changing my diaper.

I'm wearing a diaper.

I'm dreaming.

When he removes the belt across my bed and starts to slowly push me up, I automatically start to move with him as if I've done this before. Which I guess I have, in this nonsensical dream. My feet drop off the bed and I realize that I forget how to stand. I throw my torso forward awkwardly, at a loss for what my next movement should be. Tom gasps and grabs my upper arms too firmly as he pushes me back.

"Amanda, you have to remember that you haven't walked or even stood on your own yet. Please keep pace with me so you don't fall," he cautions as he puts downward pressure on my arms like a misbehaving little girl.

"'Kay," I mutter as if realizing the validity of what he's said. I know, though, that none of this is real. Once I can wake up again, everything will be normal.

What is normal?

My mind comes up blank after searching its every corner.

I let him help me into my wheelchair. As he pushes the chair out of the room and into the hall, I look toward the two doors into the dining room. I don't know where the dining room is.

But I do know where it is.

The two doors melt into one as my wheelchair approaches.

What? Oh yes, I'm dreaming.

There are three—or actually, six—others in here, two (four?) of whom are in wheelchairs. I'm forced to reduce my eyes to thin slits to make anything out of this mist.

One of them is Chris. I know this somehow. He's speaking incoherently to himself and then stops to examine me in a very uncomfortable way. He has a twin, at least until my moving wheelchair turns toward him. Now his twin dissolves into his body.

What is this?

Another, named Abdul, is yelling at an older woman as if he were having a prepubescent meltdown. He also has a doppelganger until I face him. The last is a teenage girl, Amy, who is planted on the sofa and fixated on the TV. They all have doubles until my head finds the right different angle, and I know all of their names.

What a messed up dream.

Tom pushes me up to a spot at a table I know is mine. My spot?

My head is floating on top of my body. I lack the ability to hold it upright with my neck; I can feel that much amid the excruciating pain that permeates my entire collar. Yet my head doesn't fall off as it idles inside the severely stiff and tight bracket that covers my neck, chest, and back.

What? What is going on?

The background noise of the TV feels familiar and strangely comforting. Entirely overcome, I lose myself in the hazed woodgrain of the table.

A moment, or maybe millions of moments, passes before someone sits across from me and brushes their fingertips across my knuckles. I glance up and am utterly shocked to see a cloudy image of Kyle sitting opposite me.

I know Kyle.

I am astounded that I know someone. He smiles gently and I find myself engulfed by mental images of him and a precious baby whom I know is our daughter, when just a moment ago I could recall nothing about my life.

"What… happening? Where… baby?" I whisper with agonizing slowness, searching for words, and a voice.

Kyle brushes a tear from my cheek.

"You're healing, Don." He uses a nickname I can, astonishingly, remember us calling each other. "Bailey is doing great, please don't worry about her. Your mom is taking really good care of her."

"Yes, Amanda," another voices says beside me. I'm elated to recognize that it belongs to my mom. "Bailey is healthy as a horse and as happy as ever."

In an instant, I feel devastated by absurd pain when I start to turn my head, which I can move only fractionally. I cringe in an effort not to cry out before my mom strokes my hair and puts her face in my line of obscure vision.

"Don't turn your head," she gently commands. Everything around me falls silent as I close my eyes and attempt to remember something, anything. A high-pitched hum soon accompanies the effort.

After a time without beginning or end, a narrow male face parts the fog in my mind. As it becomes clearer, this man sneers at me. The hum becomes so overbearing that I'm forced to snap out of whatever it was my mind was doing.

"Sleep?" I plead.

"Are you feeling okay? Should I go get Wade?" I couldn't tell who said it.

The mention of the nurse on the evening shift brings a face to my mind. I remember him clearly, yet I have no idea who he is. Hopeless, I shudder in miserable exhaustion.

"I… tired." Saying these words makes my fatigue more real than anything else.

I groggily start to turn over but am stopped by the sharpest shooting pain in my neck, followed by the ludicrous realization that I'm wearing some kind of extremely tight collar. Alarmed, I try to sit up, but am stopped, again, by senseless pain and a strap across my bed's side rails…

"She's been telling me she's dreaming, and when she wakes up she'll be home again. I keep telling her the truth, but it's not sinking in. She doesn't get mad; she just smiles like I'm the one in here. Is my girl going to come back?"

"No one can promise you anything, but chances are good. Amanda has come so far already. She may not ever be completely independent again, but it is obvious that she has potential to still come a long way."

Wake me up! Am I in hell?

"Oh my girl, why are you moaning? Can you hear me? Sleep, you need to sleep."

Wake me up! I don't want to sleep! What is happening?

"Sleep now. It's okay, Amanda ..."

Dreams hurt. At least waking up does, and then re-entering the forever dream that haunts me.

I pass what could be hours with my eyes closed, feigning sleep just to keep anyone from talking, if there is anyone. I don't want to know where I am.

I'm desperate to be somewhere real.

The instant I consider what reality could possibly be, I become aware of my body.

Pain. So much pain.

No.

I squeeze my eyelids resolutely, knowing that no matter what I do with my eyes, I'll be in the same place. I'll be in hell.

Somewhere is Kyle, somewhere is Bailey. My mom. They have entered my hell, and they have left. How do I leave?

Where will I be if I leave?

How do I leave?

Resentfully, with pain coursing through every part of my body and mind, I inhale. My lungs ache.

My eyes open to the Riverview room that is so condemning, I'd definitely fall into devastation if I were standing up. I'd fall anyway. I don't know how to stand up.

The distorted mass of pigment that greets my vision meets me where I am.

"Amanda, what's today's date?"

After several minutes of painful concentration under The Hum, I venture, "December 12, 2007?"

"May 26, 2009. Get with the times, girl," Wade says with a grin. "Tell me about your family, Amanda."

Family? What is family?

I struggle in desperation to draw together the images that flash through my mind continuously. The knowledge of who I am ebbs and flows in my grasp, but never flowing far enough in to fully hold onto it. Who I am and where I belong is just beyond my fingertips. The noise in my head grows to a sharp peak before the Hum fades. Beautiful faces with shocking identification flash across my internal vision.

I know these faces. These faces are my life.

Some brilliant names come to me. I am enraptured with suddenly knowing something that means everything to me.

"Bailey. My baby girl. Kyle. My... Kyle." I run out of names, but I have so many more faces. My people. Are they somewhere in this hellish nightmare? "More. Mom. Dad. More, I don't know... their names. But I know them."

Wade's smile grows with each name I squeeze out of the war room in my head. Does he know them? Of course not.

"That's great, Amanda," he cheers. "Yes, Kyle and Bailey and your parents, they love you so much. They have been here every day, all day. These names you can't remember, I know you'll know them too when I say them. Your sister Vicki. Your brother Bob and his wife Jess. Your brother Kenny and his wife Sheri." The names attach themselves to the striking faces in my head. Not just guesses. I know them. I know.

My jaw hurts really badly, I realize. When I pay attention to my own face, it dawns on me that I'm smiling. Is that what hurts?

"Does... smile..." Agonizing over every word, I finally throw out the rest of my thought. "Face hurts."

"Girl, your body went through the wringer," Wade says solemnly. "Things that shouldn't hurt are going to hurt. A lot. And probably for a while too."

Disgruntled, in agony all over, uncomfortable, confused, and mentally destitute and deficient, I close my eyes tight and sigh deeply. Pain rocks my torso when I sigh, jolting the comfort of my family out of my mind with the venomous bite in my neck that goes with it.

A weird sound escapes my mouth when I can't find a way to position my body for relief. Any way I move, something hurts, brutally.

Wade checks his watch. "It's a bit early for another dose of pain meds, but let me see what I can come up with for you. You look pretty rough."

This can't get more messed up by getting higher than I probably already am. What happens when you get high in a dream?

"No. Nothing. I'm not... normal," I answer, trying so hard to stifle the throbbing all over, along with the insanity that has swallowed me. "No pills."

Wade shakes his head. "That's noble and all, but we can't leave you in so much pain."

I know I was just barely thinking about something real. I'm sure I was. What was it, though? Someone or something so important.

There's nothing. My awareness is of nothing but what's right before my eyes.

There was something, though.

My dry throat becomes more real than any hint of recollection.

"Wade... thirsty. Water," I demand of my favourite nurse in this dream that never ends. How do I know he's my favourite? When have I seen him before? Who am I comparing him to?

"Your wish is my command." He hands me a pair of my old glasses (I have old glasses?) and I slide them onto my face. He puts a toddler-sized cup of thickened water in my hand. I have come to realize (when did I come to realize anything?) that playing along with my head trip is the only way to make the people involved treat me like I'm not insane. I'll do anything to make this unending delusion less of a nightmare.

Which people are involved, though?

"What... happening today? Something to make... normal?" I croak in my weird scratch of a voice that just won't fix itself. I think someone said my throat has been slaughtered with the procedures to monitor my collapsed, fluid-filled lungs. They say that eventually my voice will right itself. I understand only one thing: my hallucinated body and everything in it is wrecked.

Who told me? How do I know?

"Speech therapy, then lunch, then physio, then occupational therapy. Nothing your resilience can't handle," he says in an overly excited tone, knowing that speech is my most despised therapy.

Why do I hate speech therapy? What is it?

I roll my eyes and tilt my body, and therefore my brace-encased chest and neck, to reduce Wade's two left forearms to one. All this ridiculous work, just to casually punch his arm resting on my bed's side rail.

That's how to fix my double vision.

Double vision? I don't have double vision.

But I do. And I know how to correct it.

"Hey now, you know you love speech, and Miriam loves you right back. Let's get you up and out of this room."

I give Wade a sarcastic scowl as I move to the edge of the bed. I put my feet on the floor sluggishly, not quite but almost thinking about how normal people don't need to think so hard about standing up. Wade grasps my elbows and very slowly pulls me up to a stand. My jellylike legs tremble, despite him supporting all of my weight.

"Nicely done, Amanda." His gentle encouragement lifts my spirits, and I squeeze his arm in appreciation.

For a moment, I consider tightening my grip and attempting the three steps to the wheelchair, but the room quickly runs circles around me. It wouldn't have mattered if I wanted to try; Wade picks me up and brings me to the wheelchair.

"Thanks, old man," I attempt to chirp at him. I sound like the wind rushing through a forest. He pats me on the head and grins at me as he moves to turn off the TV, which I always leave on. Complete silence is torture.

When is always? I just woke up here. I always wake up here. Where is here?

"Do you know when… visit from… real world?" I try to keep my rasping voice upbeat, but I know I sound as lost as I feel.

Wade positions himself right in front of me.

"Amanda, listen to me," he demands, and pauses until my eyes meet his. "You are not dreaming. This is very real. Isn't the pain real? You have woken up like this for weeks. Nothing changes. Understand this, please."

Suddenly, truth hits me like a brick wall. Tears rush to my eyes and my breathing heaves as everything comes down on me.

"Amanda, deep breaths," Wade calmly instructs, firmly clasping my shoulders so I don't crumple and fall out of the wheelchair. A mere second's vision of a semi-truck on April 22 flashes through my mind over and over until The Hum creeps in and obliterates everything.

"Amanda, what's today's date?"

After several minutes of painful concentration under The Hum, I venture "December 18, 2007?"

"May 27, 2009 ..."

Fledgling

"AMANDA! HOW ARE YOU DOING?" LORI SQUEAKS WITH WHAT APPEARS to be honest excitement as Wade pushes my wheelchair-bound self into the physiotherapy gym.

This beautiful person gives me such a welcomed and hopeful feeling the moment our eyes meet. I know she has an endless heart. I know she will temporarily fill my soul's void with her radiant presence.

I don't know her, yet I remember her. Lori. Remember, as in I've met her... but I *haven't* met her.

This chaos is a complete delusion. People pop up into moments of my existence, and I think I know them, yet I can't remember them. I don't remember life.

I'm insane.

Obviously, this is a nightmare, that's all. It's all good.

"Okay, darling," Lori says, interrupting my psychosis. "Today, remember, we're going to get you on your feet and you're going to keep up with your incredible walking progress."

She looks me squarely in the face and has me persuaded. I feel like she could comfort me enough to walk right off a cliff.

"I started... walking?" I sift through the sieve of my memory and come up with nothing. I even come up short when I try to recall this physio gym. I give my head the tiniest shake. My neck silently screeches its protest and instantly brings me to the present.

"You stood up for a bit with support, then you dared to take a step when we were holding onto you," Lori reminds me with pride in her voice. "Today, I want you to prove me right and show yourself that you can walk with the parallel bars."

She motions to a couple of long rails beside each other. She looks at my face again, which must be displaying the terror of my heart.

"I promise, you will not be alone. I'll be right beside you. I won't take my eyes off you for a second."

Again, she looks me right in the eyes, her hands on my forearms, and I feel like I'd consider taking a stab at a jog if she asked.

I smile my consent, even while the sheer dread of what I'm agreeing to forces a tear to escape the corner of my eye. I blink the tears away fast, squeeze my eyes closed for a few seconds, and look at Lori again. Before I can reason myself away from agreeing with her, Lori grins, steps around to the back of my wheelchair, and parks me a step away from the parallel bars.

"Look at the bars, Amanda. Decide that you're going to own them, and then own them." She locks the brakes on the chair. "We're going to get you on your feet, then we'll face down those bars together."

I breathe quickly while she moves in front of me and motions to another therapist. The two stand on either side of my wheelchair and hold their arms toward me.

"Can you please take your feet out of the footrests?"

I look at my legs and think hard about moving my feet. I feel them jerk off the small platforms and drop to the floor.

That wasn't so hard. Maybe this won't be as awful as I think.

Lori kicks the wheelchair's footrests to the side and gives my arm a friendly shot, winking at me.

"Ready, Amanda?" she asks. "Find your centre, plant your feet on the floor, hold onto our forearms." She tilts her head at the other therapist. "This is Anne, by the way. Anyway, find your centre, plant your feet, grab our arms firmly, and lift yourself up."

I try to follow her instructions, but I have no idea what I'm doing.

How do I find my centre?

I picture my behind planted firmly in the chair, where it's been for as long as I can remember; planted in my wheelchair, or my bed.

Seems like enough of a centre to me.

What next?

As if reading my mind, Lori says, "Find your centre, plant your feet on the floor."

Picturing my backside, I ground my feet solidly into the floor. It feels natural to move my feet apart. As I think about and succeed at dragging them away from each other, I glance up at her in self-doubt.

She raises her eyebrows. "Look at that! Your balance is coming back. I was going to tell you to widen your base like that," she exclaims, appearing to be surprised. "The next thing that'll help your balance is to fix your eyes on one spot in front of you, like the end of one of the parallel bars right ahead."

I have to inwardly scream myself out of settling back into my seat.

Don't think about it. Just do it.

My eyes lift to the bars directly in front of me and find the end of one of them. Imagining my rear end once again, I lift my hands until they meet the arms of Lori and the other therapist. It feels too fast, but I have to keep my momentum. I lock my hands around their forearms.

Deep breath.

Lean forward.

It makes sense that when people stand, their feet hold the weight. Obviously, put some pressure on my feet. Does that make sense? Just go with it.

My body leans frontward, automatically adding force to my feet. This doesn't feel wrong. Or right.

I am terrified… and excited.

Isn't this absurdity what dreams are made of? If I'm dreaming, I might as well figure out how to stand up. Falling won't hurt me in a dream.

I pull hard on the girls' arms, putting my entire body into my feet as I start to uncurl my knees. In an instant I've nearly bowled myself over, only stopped by the therapists locking me in place with all four of their arms.

"Incredible!" Lori sings. "You're amazing!"

I'm not sure what's incredible about my body torpedoing out the wheelchair, only stopped by Lori and Anne. This is insane. What am I doing?

"No worries, Amanda, we've got you." She pushes me onward with her words. "You're finding your strength. It's fantastic! Balance your weight evenly between your legs and straighten them all the way. Lock your knees."

My knees are practically knocking together. How do I get them under control?

"Find your centre."

I don't know if Lori is talking or those words are just stuck in my head. What will that do anyway?

I picture my posterior, not knowing what else to think of as my centre. I think about where it is and how to balance it between my feet.

After some time, I feel myself growing. Is that even possible? Of course it is, I'm dreaming. Or straightening my legs completely, I realize, once I sense that my legs are stiff and have stopped shaking so hard.

Time stops. I don't move. I hardly breathe. I don't even consider taking my eyes off the end of the bar. Who knows which direction my body will go in if I look away?

"Excellent, Amanda," the other therapist softly reassures me amid this weird spell of not knowing when, how, or where to move. "Don't look away from the bar, but think about our arms for a second. We're not holding you up. You're standing on your own!"

My heart skips a beat and my breathing quickens when I recognize that there are no hands on me to keep me from falling.

"Our hands are right here," Lori jumps in. "If you start to go anywhere you shouldn't, we'll catch you. While you're on a roll, though, let's go straight ahead with the parallel bars."

They both take my hands and move them steadily to contact the bars. Once I reach them, I don't know if I've ever held onto anything so hard as these metal poles.

I chuckle at myself ruefully. What in the world am I doing trying to figure out how to walk? I'm not a toddler.

"Okay, now you're going to walk, my dear."

My eyes widen and my breathing accelerates while the therapists each put a hand beneath my elbows and onto my back.

"Move your eyes to the opposite end of this bar and focus on reaching it," Anne says. "You're going to hold onto the bars, and Lori and I will be right beside you."

Knowing that I'm being held up by two people, I dare to move my eyes to the far end of the bars. Without letting go of me, Lori and Anne step around to the outside of the parallel bars, one on each side.

"Lean to the right slightly and shift your weight to your right foot. Then, lift your left foot slowly and put it down about half a foot in front of the other." Anne puts one of her feet ahead of me. "Put your left foot down beside mine. Ready? We'll be ready to catch you if you even start to go down, promise."

She puts her hand on mine and squeezes lightly, then moves it close to my hip.

"We're going to let go of you in a few seconds. Keep your legs straight and hold the bars firmly."

My breathing catches.

"Breathe normally, Amanda, you'll do great." Lori says as she squeezes my other hand. She then holds my other hip. "Ready? We're going to let go in five seconds."

I grunt my compliance, not daring to think about it.

"Five... four... three..."

I squeeze my eyes closed for a moment and force myself to breathe.

"... two... one."

After the slightest pause, the hands holding onto my arms release me. I am alone with these two pieces of metal.

I may as well just go with this craziness. There's no point in not doing it; I'll have to figure this out eventually.

"Shift your weight to your right foot slowly, then lift your left foot."

I don't know or care who's talking anymore, I just need them to keep on doing it. I force my body to follow instructions so they keep speaking.

I have no idea how slowly or quickly I'm moving as I lean to the right, then imagine myself pushing someone else in a wheelchair instead of me being the one bound to it. I'm somehow motivated by this weird thought, and I fractionally lift my left foot. I wait for myself to fall, but I don't.

Confused and excited, I haltingly lift my foot another inch, then another.

Put it down about half a foot in front of the other.

I hope I'm remembering real instructions, and this isn't just another crazy idea floating around in my head. I jerk my foot forward and snap it down to the floor so fast that I wait for myself to fall.

Nothing. I don't fall.

I tighten my grip on the bars, even though it already feels like my hands are going to squeeze dents into them. I force my eyes to follow the parallel bars back toward me until they meet my white-knuckled hands, then travel down my legs to my feet. My left foot is a few inches in front of my right and I'm still standing.

The weirdest sensation of delight mixed with irritation washes over me. I giggle in morbid amusement. What's wrong with me?

I slowly notice that Lori and Anne are talking to me.

"Amanda! This is great!"

"Don't stop. You've got it!"

My eyes follow the path back up my body and down the bars, to the end opposite me.

What now?

"Now move your hands forward, one at a time. Lean to the left, exactly the same as how you just leaned to the right. Then move your right foot forward the same way."

These girls have this uncanny ability to read my mind.

I shift my weight to the left, but stabilizing hands on that side of my back and hip tell me I've moved too far and too fast. I don't have the capacity to figure out which therapist is on that side as she firmly pushes me back to an upright position.

"Try that one more time, Amanda."

I take a shallow breath and move guardedly to the left again. When I stop and feel my weight centred on my left foot, I swiftly lurch the other foot into the air and snap it forward and down with a forceful exhalation.

"Great. Now can you slow down and move your feet ahead more steadily?"

Whoever's talking fades out as my mind runs circles around my barely functioning legs. I picture myself walking out of this illogical place.

I can't even fathom what I'd walk out to, but I need to be anywhere but here.

I'm heaved out of my escape fantasy by sudden tight grips on my elbows.

"You've got to stay focused, my dear," Lori says as she and Anne force me to rise to my full height. Without even noticing, I guess I started going down.

I can't leave. I can't even think about something else without biting the ground. For what feels like the millionth time, my eyes get hot with this realization of complete dependence on others, even though I can't actually pinpoint any one of those times.

"Let's give this another go," Anne says. "Don't think so hard. You're getting this so much faster than anyone thought."

I feel wetness leak from my eyes. Feeling their grip, I dare to lower my eyes from their focus point to my pathetic feet.

"We can get you back to the chair to have a quick breather if you want," she continues.

This is insanity. My feet can move; they just showed me that. How can I not control my own limbs enough to keep going?

No. These are my own legs. This is my body. It does what I tell it to. This can't happen.

"No," I hiss at myself. "I am not sitting down."

Lori and Anne both suck in air as if they're shocked. I'm not sure if they're playfully exaggerating, and it only aggravates me more.

I grip the bars rigidly once again and shake their hands off.

Don't think. Just go. I force my eyes to find their previous target.

Lean one way. Lift the other foot. Move it forward, put it down. Move hands forward. Repeat. As my legs and arms carry out the instructions from my thoughts, I feel removed from myself. I hardly sense that I'm moving until my hands reach the end of the bars, and my perception hurls itself back into my body. A cocktail of emotions washes through all of me: celebration, mourning, joy, rage, calmness, agitation.

Eventually, I hear the hoots and hollers of the whole therapy gym. Lori is calling out to the entire company of therapists and fellow rehab inmates.

"Ladies and gentleman, we have a walker here!"

Unable

THE CLOCK TICKS. IT TICKS AND TOCKS, YET THE HANDS NEVER MOVE. I sleep and awaken, and the hands crawl just fractionally during my relentlessly echoing dreams. Then I open my eyes to this undying nightmare.

I have to pee. The quest to get to the bathroom and back should kill off some gaps between the numbers on that cursed clock. In the same amount of time it would take any normal person to get out of bed and use the bathroom, I grab the bed's rails, sit up in disgustingly slow motion, painfully inch my way to a sitting position, and warily lower my feet to the floor. My feet are cinder blocks when they hit the ground. The shaking of my legs seems heightened under time-warped tension as I awkwardly, sluggishly lift myself to stand. Deliberately, I hold onto the bedrail behind me and lean forward as far as I dare, slit my eyelids, and painstakingly decode the neon green blur that is the time on the digital clock in front of me.

At the same time as I gape over the revelation that time appears to have moved backwards by five minutes, my head drifts into the familiar spiral that always sends me to my knees.

"No," I whisper in desperation, my mind pushing away the looming shutdown. Battling to stay on my feet, I force my lungs to exchange air at a steady pace, even while I'm trembling so hard the room seems to be quaking.

I don't shift out of my position for an eternity for fear that everything, including me, will fall.

"Amanda. Amanda, can you hear me?"

The soft voice shatters my severe focus on something I can't even name. I tighten my grip on the bed and inhale slowly. I should have put my glasses on before attempting anything like what I'm doing.

The shape in the doorway has the voice of someone I know, but who?

"You're standing up. By yourself. That is amazing," the familiar voice says softly, as if to avoid startling me. She moves toward me slowly like someone approaching a wet cat.

That voice... whose voice is that? My mind runs through the female knowledge it holds. My mom, Lori—

Oh! I remember.

"Sheri?" I ask timidly, hopeful for familiarity, embarrassed for incompetence. There are so many things wrong with me.

"Yes! Amanda, it's me!" she somehow manages to shriek in a half-whisper.

Sheri scurries to my side.

One of my sisters. I have sisters? Sheri. One more? No, two more.

Someone else is shuffling up behind her, and then there's a second set of hands on my unsupported arm. When I move my eyes in this new person's direction, they meet two new sets of eyes: two more sisters. I knew it.

I knew it?

I'm astonished to have managed to stay on my feet while thinking about something else, and at the same time extremely annoyed that I'm in a state to be amazed by something like that.

After a long halt, it finally occurs to me that I have three visitors in the room with me.

"Jess? Vicki?" I finally throw out breathlessly, focusing hard on the floor. I can't look at them. If I do, I'll hit the floor faster than I woke up in this nightmare.

So many arms surround my back as they take a gentle but firm grip on me.

"It's us. Amanda, we're here."

"Oh, I'm so relieved you know us!"

"Amanda!"

It doesn't even matter who's talking to me. There is just so much solace in the fact that someone is here. Not just someone, three people. People who I know. I didn't even know I knew them.

"Were you going to the bathroom?" one of them asks.

"Yeah," I chuckle bitterly after a long process to recall what my body is telling me it needs to do. "Been on my way for... hours... probably."

"I'm so proud of you for doing it alone, but can you please buzz a nurse next time?" Jess squeezes my arm. "I know you could do it on your own. You could for sure, but if you doubt yourself, you could let yourself fall. Let's go."

She says it in a way that doesn't make me feel like an idiot as she ushers me into a nearby wheelchair and pushes me toward the bathroom.

Did I actually just attempt to go somewhere on my own? Did I really not hit the ground right away?

A petrifying, brilliant idea takes root in my mind.

No way. I couldn't do that.

My crazy does have a reasonable side. I can't do it.

But…

That's exactly what I need to do. There's nothing else I can do.

I'm going to walk out of here when no one is looking.

Extremely liberated at the same time as petrified, this insane thought grows exponentially. I'm trapped in some kind of gateway to hell, where people randomly come visit me but don't take me out with them when they leave. I have to get out of here. How much longer before these people throw me into a padded cell?

"Amanda. Where are you, babe?" Sheri asks as she nudges the bathroom door open.

I blink fast in an attempt to focus on the task at hand. Bathroom. Standing up, walking. One foot in front of the other.

"Trying not to fall." The half-truth cushions my conscience.

I'm not lying. Just not telling her everything. I'm learning how to lie. Is that progress?

I mentally shake my head.

"You're doing really well. I'm so proud of you, Amanda," someone says, putting a hand on my shoulder. "Let's get this done. I can see you're getting spent out here already."

Gateway from Hell

"I HAVE THE BIGGEST SURPRISE IN THE WORLD FOR YOU, AMANDA," Wade announces with flair as he moves my wheelchair down the hall.

I don't have the slightest idea how to respond. Surprise? Every moment of my life is an utterly perplexing shock, even while I have no choice but to stay locked up right where I am. I chuckle nervously as I envision him rolling the chair up to the wide open door of a padded cell.

Wade brings us around a couple of corners and one floor down on an elevator.

Remember this. I might need this.

He pushes me through an opening into a small square room with double doors—and what appears to be *outside* on the other side of them.

This can't be. I adjust my glasses and angle my torso in a way that rectifies the mess of my vision.

The front doors of this prison lay before me. Doors I haven't known the location of before. Doors, and the path we just took, that I try in earnest to burn into my brain.

There's a world outside of this hellish building.

"Ready, girl?" Wade interrupts in his good-humoured way.

I can never stop myself from grinning at him; that's all I do. I can't make myself form a single word. He presses the wall switch, the doors swing open, and he eagerly glides me forward. Instead of hitting some phantom wall like I imagine, the wheelchair crosses the threshold with me still in it. And then it keeps on going.

I am outside. I am not confined in Riverview.

I am outside.

I gasp for air before I realize I've been holding my breath. Wade animatedly thumps my upper arm and keeps walking across the pavement.

"Here we are. Nature. The world. Welcome back." He turns off the parking lot, onto a path that winds through trees and down a slope. I don't know what to look at. There's so much more than four walls and a forever-ticking, never-moving clock. No nurses, doctors, or therapists, but *life*. Colour. Movement. Beautiful noise.

I close my eyes and inhale as slowly and fully as I can. There is no stale Riverview flavour to this brilliant gulp of air. Just pure, unadulterated oxygen. I hardly feel the throbbing that always goes with breathing deeply. I feel high with the aching beauty of the outside world.

"Amanda!" Wade's childishly excited voice pulls me out of the blinding fog of my thoughts. "Look up. That's the Red River up there!"

As we move down a paved walkway, I strain my eyes in desperate pursuance of the river he speaks of. When I see it ahead of me, I am entranced. I hardly blink for an eternity, unable to tear my eyes away from the captivating sight of moving water.

I start to drop my head back in an elated trance but am stopped short, as always, by agonizing pain and my neck brace. My eyes water while my neck throbs razor blades, and I know Wade is saying something.

But I just don't care.

There is a world outside of my hell. There is a way out. Nature is real, not just a figment of my insane imagination.

Although, as senseless as this whole affliction has been, how can I possibly know if this is real? Is this just another insult to my soul? I'll probably wake up to the kiss of death in my Riverview bed again, or worse, truly open my eyes to hell.

"What's going on in that head of yours?"

"Uh, amazing," I whisper after mentally scrambling for a word that doesn't scream paranoia. "Thank you."

Wade laughs under his breath. "What's amazing is that we could have probably just put you and your bed outside instead of pumping you full of painkillers," he jokes, probably referring to me practically breaking my neck again just a moment ago and hardly realizing it.

Whoa. Did I just think of something that happened before this very moment I'm in right now?

Before my crazy mind can own me again, I force out the beginning of a question that I'm sure I've asked millions of times already, but I can't recall any sort of reassurance about.

"Wade." I can't get any words past my throat, but Wade waits. "Wade."

I pause for another moment; still he waits. I'm sure he's anticipating my words.

I close my eyes and with the expectation of absolutely nothing, and everything at the same time, I squeak, "Is there an end to this? If this is real, when can I be... normal? When can I... go... home? When... when?"

I run out of words, just like the hope I've run out of, in a life I can't even really remember.

In an unsettling moment of déjà vu, Wade sinks to eye level in front me and very firmly states, "Amanda, you are not dreaming. You will leave this place. You have come so far, and you have to know that this is as real as it gets. I swear you will walk out of here. Maybe in a month, maybe two months..."

He loses my eyes as soon as he says I've come so far, and I can't bring myself to look back at him. What a despicable lie. I have not come far. I can't walk without parallel bars or someone to hold onto for dear life, and therefore I can't walk out of here. I feel like I can recall some official-looking person saying that I may or may not ever walk unassisted again.

"Ah, well... with a wheelchair... or not... I will leave." Silently I add, *Soon.*

"Yes! Amanda! That's what I want to hear out of you! You got it, girl," he yelps with a gusto that brings a fast smile to my stone cold face. "Be determined. Be brave. Be unshakeable." The passion and confidence in his voice is unreal.

It can't be real. He can't have this kind of honest excitement when he's talking about me. First, this may or may not be actually happening, so there's nothing genuine about it anyway. Second, I'm a gimp. What is there to be confident about?

Yet this incredible person seems surreal in an angelic way that makes the tone of everything he says perfectly suited to him. It's almost as if God put Wade in this rehab hospital, at this time, to be here specifically for my senseless mind.

Wade says I'll walk out of here. He says I'm fine. I'm not crazy, not dreaming this insanity.

Whether or not this is real, I have to get out of here.

I'll show myself that I can walk out of here.

Soon.

Contrivance

"YOU... GO. I'M... OKAY," I TELL KYLE WITH ALL THE NORMALITY I CAN maintain. When he has to leave, it requires a lot of reassurances and promises to return before I let him go. One of these days, when I open my eyes, he and my family won't be here anymore, and my dream will finally become the hell I know it really is.

I have to do this before that happens.

Kyle approaches me with wide eyes. "Really? I don't even need to leave for another hour. I can stay for a bit."

His wariness rattles my already shaky confidence. I quickly close my eyes. Before I can beg him to stay like I desperately want to, I feign the courage that everyone wants me to have, and which I need for my intended scheme.

"Everyone says... do this. I need to let go... whatever," I mutter in a mocking tone. "Not a dream. Right? You'll come back. You won't disappear."

Everything in me screams not to let him go. This time, he will actually be gone. My nightmare will finally reveal its true blackness and I'll be alone.

If my escape plan doesn't work.

I swallow my heart, and in the most even voice I can muster, I announce, "I can do this."

He stands in front of me and, gently holding both of my arms, kisses my forehead. "I'm proud of you, Don. I'll be back tomorrow after work, I promise."

He kisses my forehead again and looks into my eyes intently, as if waiting for me to laugh and squeak, "Just kidding!" He lets go of me seconds before my trembling gets violent enough to give me away.

He rests his hand on the side of my face for a moment. "Love you."

I need a delay. I can't let him go. I'll never see him again. I squeeze my eyes shut and take a deep breath in the most natural way I can manage. I swallow over and over in an attempt to relieve my dry mouth. I finally force a smile and look up at the angel of my dream.

"Love you," I say. "Come back."

He kisses me soundly on the mouth and takes slow steps backwards toward the door. He pauses, puts his fist over his heart (his way of promising to return), and then my cornerstone leaves me forever.

Convicted

I FEEL MYSELF DRIFTING FROM SLEEP TO WAKEFULNESS. GHOSTS OF memories that I just can't quite grasp swirl through my mind. I keep my eyes closed, willing myself to wake up at home. Pain permeates my body, but I desperately hold onto the idea that if I try hard enough, I'll wake up in a safe haven without a scratch. I hear footsteps nearby and pray it's not a nurse or therapist or someone else to show me I'm still in my dream within a dream.

"Mama night-night."

The tiny, sweet voice of my girl brings a smile to my face. I don't open my eyes, imagining I'm in my own bed with my baby beside me. A pint-sized hand rubs my hair. I clasp it as if it's holding my very existence. Whoever's holding her starts to put her by my side, but she whimpers when they try to let go of her.

"No no no!"

Hot tears slip beneath my eyelids at her urgent demand to not be left beside me. She doesn't know what I am to her.

"Bailey, your mommy loves you. She wants to be with you every day, I promise," my mom's voice murmurs.

Wretchedly accepting that I'll open my eyes to Riverview once again, I give in. Bailey smiles at me from a safe distance, back in my mom's arms. I return it as much as I can through my tears.

"Hi monkey," I whisper, tears streaming. I clear my throat, wipe my eyes, and give Mom a half-smile. "Hi Mom. I told you … wake me up. Why are you letting me sleep so long?"

"Amanda, do you mean to tell me you still think you're dreaming? Even after last night?" Her intensity catapults my paranoia. I stare at her, the question written on my face. "You tried to escape. You sent Kyle home and tried to waltz—well, hobble while holding onto the wall—out of here!"

"You ... kidding me? I can't even walk like a normal person. Nowhere to go. Why would I?" I challenge, even knowing that my mind doesn't hold onto most things for long. It obviously could have happened.

Mom rubs her temples before sitting down at eye level. She manages to force eye contact.

"Don't ever do that again." She looks up, collecting herself before going on. "You scared us all to death. You have a little girl and a very committed fiancé to get better for. You will not get better on the streets of Winnipeg with no one knowing where you are. You couldn't even get as far as the streets. And without your neck brace? You have no idea how badly you could have hurt yourself permanently. They're not sure how this has affected your spine's healing, or how much it set you back."

Mom's rant ends abruptly as she covers her distraught face with her free hand.

"Please," she chokes through her fingers. "Stay here, accept the fact that this is for real, and give it your all."

I close my eyes in an attempt to let sleep swallow me again. I don't open them. This has to change at some point. If I try hard enough, if I will it hard enough, maybe I can wake up in the real world.

My eyes stay closed for a long time. It all feels the same, though.

Finally, I force myself to pretend to believe this is actually not some deranged head trip.

My mind's barricade breaks after some time, and a flood of tears escapes with the notion that I might have to plough through a long recovery. Having no idea what that will involve, I clam up again.

Somehow, I recognize that crying in front of Bailey won't help her smile, so I rein in my sobs as quickly as they escaped.

"This is ... real, isn't it," I mutter in more of a statement than a question. "Hell on earth, Mom."

"I know, Amanda," she whispers, stroking Bailey's cheek. "It's misery for all of us. We almost lost you. But we didn't. Now we thank God for your life, and you need to give this your all. Bailey needs you."

Bailey leans into Mom's hand while she stares at me. I can almost hear her tiny voice pleading with Mom to never leave her with me. My heart bleeds.

I pick up a photo album off the bedside table. I flip the pages until I find a picture of Bailey giving me a kiss. I hold the album out to Mom.

"Show her."

Mom takes it and holds the album up to Bailey.

"Look, Bailey! Who's that?" she asks, pointing at the picture.

"Baby," Bailey answers with a giggle.

"Who's baby kissing?"

"Baby," Bailey repeats, pointing at herself.

"Who's holding baby?"

"No, no, baby! Baby!" Bailey insists, banging on the picture with her fist.

I recall suddenly that Bailey can be very stubborn—and the memory gives me a brief moment of jubilee. But the knowledge that my little girl doesn't depend on me anymore shatters me again. I bury my face in my hands for a minute, ten minutes, I have no idea. How is it that of the few memories I have, the most precious one is the one who avoids me with all she has?

Mom puts her free hand on my knee and gives me a sympathetic squeeze. I freeze.

Why am I crying?

What just happened?

"Mom, I don't know—"

I stop myself when I see Bailey staring back at me.

Oh yes, I was ruined by my daughter's disownment of me. That's what happened. I cannot force my eyes away from hers as I process the knowledge that, one, my baby girl does not know me anymore; two, I'm a brain-damaged mess in a mental hospital; and three, I'm dreaming all this but cannot wake up.

Who is really taking care of Bailey while I'm in some kind of eternal sleep? Where am I really? What am I missing in my actual life while I'm trapped in purgatory?

"Amanda, what are you thinking about?" Mom's voice cuts into my haunted musings.

I blink hard and look toward her voice. My eyes find hers and I somehow see past everything to the terror that torments this beautiful woman.

I can't even dream of the sort of emotion harboured behind my mother's eyes.

This can only be real. What else can it be?

Seeing me crumble in revelation all over again, Mom's face falls. She places Bailey on the bedside chair with her cell phone to stop the protests before they begin, then perches on the edge of my bed and cups my face above the neck brace.

"Amanda, I love you so much, and you have an army fighting this with you. God is all around you. He'll bring you as far as you let Him. Please, please don't lose hope before you even find it," she murmurs, wiping at my tears with her thumbs. "Can Pastor Glen help you wrap your head around this? Do you remember him?"

Pastor Glen, Pastor Glen. My mind tosses around this name for a long moment and then picks up a face to accompany it.

"He has been here for you a lot," Mom says with a smile in her voice. "Right from when you were in intensive care the day this happened. He was going to marry you and Kyle. He's very dear to our family."

My mind holds no knowledge of him, other than the fluke awareness that he's the pastor at the church my family attends. I am momentarily thrilled to realize I'm remembering two things at once: a person and a place that are both important to my family. The thrill is immediately dashed with the understanding that such an influential person is seeing me at my absolute worst. And then some.

"Pastor Glen was here just yesterday, and then a few days before that," Mom continues, trying to spark some memory. "He comes often, and he always makes you smile. He'll be back here on Monday again."

As I try to recover a conversation with Pastor Glen in my memory, I become aware of what feels like static electricity running through my left arm. I can't feel my hand. I pinch it.

I feel almost nothing.

"Mom, can't… feel… hand. Arm… tingling," I whisper. I'm so tired of talking. My neck feels like acid is coursing through it.

Mom presses a bright red button on the side of my bed at the same time as she grabs the hand closest to her.

"Other one," I mumble. She reaches for my left hand as Wade enters the room.

"What's going on, ladies?" Wade asks casually, although his voice is tinted with concern.

"She says her hand is numb and her arm is tingling," Mom squeaks.

What's wrong with my arm? Is numbness bad?

"I'll call Dr. Johnson." He spins on his heel and leaves the room.

I rub my wrist, the back and front of my hand, and my forearm.

Or am I? I feel next to nothing on my arm, and nothing at all on my hand. Mom takes a deep breath and moves to easy eye contact with me.

"Amanda, that stunt you pulled with your neck brace was very dangerous," she says in a thin voice. "This is more real than anything. You are not dreaming. You just can't do things like take off your brace and try to leave. Can you please tell me you understand this?"

I stare at the blurry image that is my mother. My mother, who comes into my nightmare with my baby girl. My child, my lifeline, who doesn't even know me. Me, who doesn't know where, how, what, when, or who exactly I am.

How did I get here? What did I come from?

What was I doing the moment before I became a ghost in a prison world?

My mom forgotten, I stare vacantly at the TV while my awareness drifts from my state of quarantine, to fragments of my life. My daughter, Kyle, Mom, Vicki, Sheri, and Jess (maybe Sheri and Jess, or did I just imagine them?) are at the tip of that iceberg. The rest of my existence, that I can't quite see, is a mass beneath the surface of my turbulent mind.

I know Mom is talking. I don't hear a word. The Hum is looming, but I push back. I gouge the wall in my head with everything in me. Frustration, fury, irritation, and every other emotion encompass me while I throw daggers at the barrier.

In some otherworldly view and sensation, I am suddenly cradled in an overpowering hold, though it's also gentler than the softest summer breeze. All of me is at rest. My furious mind game doesn't even exist.

Never will I leave you; never will I forsake you.

Not vocalized, not seen, but I know these words are being spoken to the depths of my core. Even while I know that my body is writhing in pain, discomfort, and captivity, I don't feel anything. These ten words have more weight than anything else in the world.

There will be a day with no more spiritual, mental, and physical pain, but until that day I'll be here. Maybe not here, stuck in Riverview, but here in this terrifying and erratic life. Right now, in this moment, I know this. I know it, and I'm at peace with it. Inch by inch, the black night of my soul is streaked with understanding, and the dawning of hope.

I start to feel myself being pulled away from this brilliant pause in my nightmare. Instead of bracing myself for the onslaught of aching confusion, I feel calm. Focusing on Mom, I see her precious face filled with concern, yet wrapped in serenity.

"I see that you are getting pretty tired, so you go to sleep. I'm going to run to the store to grab you something to read," Mom says with the kindness etched into her whole being.

"Mom, thank you." I say it in the most normal voice I've heard come out of my mouth since I've been here. Whatever just happened has lifted my brain out of a dark hole. Mom stops putting on her sweater for a second and furrows her brow. Then she grins and pulls up the zipper.

"For what?" She brushes my hair out of my face with her free hand.

"For being… here. Being… you." I scratch out the words like a skipping disc. The war on my mind was only given the briefest ceasefire, I guess.

And yet I feel hope.

Someone is with me. Someone who is bigger than me. Or Mom. Or anyone.

Echoes

I INHALE DEEPLY, CLOSE MY EYES, PAUSE, EXHALE. A GREY CLOUD vacates my open mouth. I laugh at something, or someone. I lift a glass and take a swig of burning, sweet liquid; lift a long glass tube to my lips, put the flame of a lighter against a bowl at the end of the tube, inhale deeply again. A beautiful ache swathes my lungs and becomes electric as it spreads to the rest of me. Exhale again.

A tiny white line of powder captivates me the moment I look at it. Someone hands me a rolled-up dollar bill. I ravenously and clumsily take it and position the bottom of the bill to one end of the white line, lower my left nostril to the top of the rolled-up bill. I press a finger to the other nostril, close my mouth, and inhale slowly and strongly as I move the tube of money along the line of powder.

My body jerks me out of a restless sleep with a twitch that lifts me off the bed for a split second. I hardly give a thought to the sensation of a knife impaling my neck.

What was that?

I feel resonances of something like... painful complacency.

I just had a dream that was definitely not just another insane delusion to complete my already irrational state. I haven't even been aware of this former life until this moment, but I know I just saw a big part of my existence.

I had a memory.

Gallons of alcohol. Cocaine, crack, meth… vices that paint a big, abstract picture of elated misery in my mind. I recall many instances where I was frozen in moments higher than mountain peaks.

I shudder violently. My prior life hasn't existed until this point in time. Now it exists, but still only in the form of dependence. Always needing something to hold me up, even before this mess I've woken up in where I am fully dependent on so many things and so many people. Back then, whenever that was, I could move and walk and talk all I wanted, but I created a gross dependence for myself that was fully selfish and stupid.

What else was there to my life? I must have been a decent, functional human being at some point. How long has that life been anyway? I don't even know how old I am.

I search the plane of my mind beyond the repulsive knowledge of myself it houses. Besides the feeling of knowing I broke my own and my parents' hearts relentlessly, I come up blank. At this point, there's nothing more to me than always needing some sort of crutch.

I don't realize I'm heaving a deep sigh, but it lands me back in the present, in my bed, with the lung ache that springs off it. I groan and raise my hand to my chest, where it meets the plastic that's always in the way. I press my hand into my brace as hard as I can to feel some sort of resistance.

I hate this. I can't do anything for myself. I can't even move in the right way to give my body some relief. Can't bend over to scratch an itch on my leg. Can't get up and take a two-minute walk to wake up a sleeping foot.

A sudden recognition of tingling in my left arm reminds me of something. Something happened… yesterday? My fingers flex in slow motion and stop before they're fully straight. Focusing hard, I try willing them straight, only succeeding after an amount of time I shouldn't even need to think about. It should have just happened, but it didn't.

I give my head a miniscule shake and think back. I know something happened to make my arm weird like this.

Oh!

Apparently I tried to get out of this hellish place. They say I took off my neck brace and tried to walk out. After that, my arm went numb. How is that connected, though?

"Good morning, Amanda," Wade greets cheerfully as he strides into the room. His expression falls slightly as he studies my face.

"Morning, Wade," I barely whisper.

He lowers himself into the bedside chair and glances at me before looking out the window and studying the view past the glass. After a few moments, it becomes clear that he's waiting for me to talk.

"I think I'm remembering stuff," I start, then stop. I can't even find words to describe what's going through my head.

"This is... all so... wrong. I feel like... I dream, or see in my head stuff that is never... good. I can't put... memories together. I have no idea how long, or if this was actually me... between stuff that... pops into my head." I feel like I'm about to break a sweat; it's so hard to even vocalize such a long thought that I don't fully understand. Before I can think more about how to say it, I toss out, "I think I used to do coke and meth and a lot more drugs."

I stare a hole into my fully mobile right hand, forcing my handicapped left fingers to curl into a tight ball. I feel Wade looking at me. He probably thinks I'm an ungrateful, stupid swine for ever doing garbage like meth. He doesn't say anything. He despises me.

I jump slightly when his hand lands softly on mine. He then crosses his arms and sits back.

"You remember," he says. "You look like you saw a ghost, so I can obviously see that you know you made a few wrong moves in your lifestyle choices."

I look at Wade. There is no condemnation on his face. Even while I'm relieved that he doesn't seem to hate me for my stupidity, I'm so ashamed. I look away again.

"I promise... if I find myself, I'll never, never do that again," I state, feeling an intense need to rectify Wade's view of me.

"Girl, don't promise me that. Promise yourself that." He grins. "I know you're good. I know that. And when you find yourself again, because there are no ifs about it, I know you'll do big things. Awesome things. And besides, before you landed in here, by the sounds of it, you were cleaned up and an awesome mom. So even though you don't remember just yet, there's more to you than meets your mind's eye." Wade smiles again, then clears his throat as his face becomes stern. "You're a good kid, but Amanda. You did something that might very well have set you way back." His voice goes hard with these words. "Your CTO was definitely not ready to come off. You took it off. You can't do that."

The CTO stands for cervical thoracic orthosis, a brace designed to immobilize the cervical and upper thoracic spine.

"What do you mean?" I have been told this. I remember being told this. I remember that I even thought of this a few moments ago. Yet I don't recall doing it. This is insane.

"You took off the brace and tried to leave. Never mind trying to leave. You took the brace off. Your neck isn't ready for that. You could have permanently lost your arm's full function."

"No way... I don't remember doing that!" I almost yell, despite my ability to hardly speak past a whisper. I've been told that I did exactly that, but I can't remember doing it. I suck as a human being. I'm not even a human being. Who can't remember giving themselves a handicap, pretty much on purpose?

"You did it; Tom stopped you. You got as far as the nurse's desk on this floor. But now we can't say where this leaves you. There's no way to treat the type of damage this may have caused. You might have given yourself an incomplete spinal cord injury, or basically, your arm might be out of luck for good."

Wade rubs his temples and releases his pinched eyebrows slowly.

My heart is exhausted by this emotional hurricane, shifting from nightmares to rediscovering abhorrent memories for the first time, to self-hatred, to being accepted so fully by someone I respect fiercely, to receiving a firm reprimand from that same person... all of it, within minutes, is completely draining. This just gets more and more crazy. Or I get more and more crazy.

I curse under my breath and rub my face hard with one hand. I need to wake myself up. How long can this terror last?

"Wade. This is sick. Wake me up."

"You know you're not dreaming. As much as you want this to be a dream, you know it's not."

"One can hope," I mumble. I could very well wake up in the next moment. But I keep on not waking up.

"I can only imagine," Wade says. "I'm sure it's messed up to suddenly be stuck like this and not remember a whole lot. But you've got to decide to get past it. You're not going anywhere until you make up your mind to get somewhere."

"Yada, yada." I roll my eyes. "I think I know you're right. But I still... feel like I'm right. This is the stuff of bad dreams."

Wade shrugs, nods, and smiles like he always does. "Well, you're just going to have to fix yourself right up again like you would in a dream, right? Also, did you hear yourself speak just now? You're putting thoughts into words! You're on your way up."

Whoa. I spoke like a normal person. I wasn't even thinking about it. Maybe I just need to stop thinking so hard. How, though?

"Amanda, Dr. Johnson says only time will tell if your arm's fine or not. But until time opens her mouth, we're just going to plough through and get you on your feet."

He drops my shoes on the floor beside my bed and nods at Lori, who steps into the room, followed by Anne.

Anne? I know her name. As has become the custom, I guess I know her.

Oh yeah, I remember Anne. Physio. Lori and Anne. With a painfully cavernous breath, I slide my hands up on the bed beside me and push myself up, more with my right arm than my tingly left one. By the time I'm sitting up, my abdomen and back ache and my arms—or at least one of them—feel like I've just lifted a fifty-pound dumbbell. I blink to focus on the faces around me and am greeted by three slack-jawed expressions.

Lori recovers herself, probably because of my own confused face. She moves toward me swiftly and lays her hand on my arm.

"Do you even realize what you just did?" Her beaming face and mile-high eyebrows confuse me even more. She's not unhappy or concerned. I might even say she's delighted.

It gradually occurs to me that I'm sitting up. Not only that, but I sat up without thinking about what I was doing. Like it was natural. Like I was a functional, adult, sane human being for a few seconds. I feel my mouth curve into a smile.

· *Never will I leave you.*

My neck screams as I move my head to find the source of these words. I ignore the scream, though, still smiling like an idiot even when I know that no person has spoken to me. As crazy as I may be, trapped in my mind game, I feel like this tranquil voice belongs to someone I need to trust.

"Look at you, sitting and moving your head around like you own the place," Wade squawks in mock protest, bringing me back to the present.

The vice grip around and inside my spine doesn't seem to have loosened; I just pushed my neck past its limit enough to shrink my eyelids to twitching, teary messes while I was in some brief invincible state.

"I thought I heard something," I whisper in a quivering voice, even while smiling with anticipation. I've pretty much reduced myself to tears, but if I can force myself so far on accident, how far can I go if I really try? "I wasn't really… thinking about it. I feel it now, though, for sure. What does that even mean?"

Lori takes both of my hands in hers. "Girl, you will walk right out of here when the time's right, and you're getting closer to that point. What you just showed us is that if you don't overthink it, you can go a lot farther than you give yourself credit for. You sat up like you would have before you landed up in here, and you turned your head a couple inches farther than you have yet." My smile only grows as she keeps talking, but Lori seems suddenly wary of my face. "You cannot try to leave again, though, Amanda. That would probably put you back at square one. Do you feel your arm?"

"I swear, I'm only happy because I feel… hopeful. Someone is helping me. I feel like I can get better." Even my words are coming out easier all of a sudden.

"That's my girl! You can get better. I love this!" Lori whoops. "Should we go for a walk? I came in here to give you some grief for trying to bail on us," she winks at me, "but it seems like we should just carry on and get you on your way out of here."

As I move my gaze toward my feet, my eyes stop at the sight of my left hand. My moments-ago soaring confidence evaporates.

"Is that okay for my arm?" I question, suddenly bashful.

"We can't do anything about that. But keep on living. That will have to heal in its own time, if it heals at all. Get the rest of your body up to speed, and hopefully your arm will follow suit."

Never will I leave you.

I twitch slightly at these words. Am I imagining them? I bite my lips to keep from asking if anyone else heard them. I know they didn't.

"Okay, I'm ready. Let's go." I shuffle to the edge of the bed, drop my legs off the side, and put my feet on the floor. Without making eye contact with any one of the three around me, I lift my hands and smile. "Someone going to help me up?"

After a beat, Wade bellows with amusement, "Keep this up and we'll just toss you outside and watch you laugh as you get up and walk away from us."

Anne pushes a wheelchair beside me and the girls both take my lifted hands, squeezing them hearteningly. Feeling their arms stiffen and grips tighten, I summon a mental picture of myself rising to stand.

"Think of what we went over in therapy last time to get you standing up," Lori says. "Do you remember?"

"Yes."

"Ready?"

"Yes."

"You own this, woman! Three, two, one, up."

After a brief pause, I picture my rear end right between my feet, then lean forward slowly and put weight into my base. Without allowing myself shock and wonder at my unexpected and alien capability, I find myself rising to as full a height as I can manage.

"Wow," I breathe, taken off guard by the strange mix of pain and relief in my trunk.

"Amanda!"

"Yes! Yes!"

Anne and Lori hoot jubilantly at the same time. Wade just chuckles. I can picture the wry expression on his face.

The liberty of standing up without the meticulous coaching it took last time has me feeling so much less vulnerable than even a minute ago.

"More," I say. "Let's do more. I need more."

Their quiet, excited laughter is accompanied by their rigid arms rising up alongside me. I firmly take hold of them, lean to the left, coax my right foot forward, and repeat on the other side.

Keeper

BAILEY'S FACE. BAILEY'S TINY HANDS. BAILEY'S SWEET VOICE.

Bailey's cries. My daughter's cries.

I reach toward my baby, but my hands never touch her. I stretch farther. I stretch until every inch of me screams with the burning length to which I've distended my body. My Bailey, my baby, is just beyond my fingertips. Crying, screaming, I rip myself in half to get to her, but I can't do it. My massing shrieks only tear her farther out of reach, and she falls beyond the realm of my vision.

"Bailey... Bailey..." I hear myself mumble.

A soft hand on my cheek breaks up my misery. I peel my eyes apart and am struck with confused relief to see my beautiful, precious mom. Blinking back tears in my eyes confuses me further. Why am I crying?

Sitting on the side of my bed, Mom bends down and plants a kiss on my forehead. When she sits up again, her eyes smile along with her mouth. She is an angel. My angel slides my glasses onto my face.

"Hi sweetheart. Bailey is safe. They're taking good care of her at daycare during the day until you get home to do that. I drop her off there in the morning and pick her up in the afternoon. Don't worry; she'll be waiting for you when you come home."

My breathing catches. "Mom, how do you always know what I'm thinking?"

People seem to be reading my mind everywhere.

She smiles empathetically. "You're a mom. I'm a mom. I know your heart. And you were saying her name in your sleep."

"I'm always sleeping, though. Even now. This is a dream." Although I think I might be wrong and I know she'll tell me otherwise.

Mom just shakes her head at me, the smile in her eyes not waning despite my senselessness. She pushes my ever-straying, unwashed hair off my forehead and twists it away from my face in an effort to restrain it. After some time, she speaks.

"It sounds like you're starting to think this could be the real thing. Which it is. I have to know, though, what makes you think that?"

Dreary images flash through my mind with Mom's question, accompanied by jubilation at this newfound ability to remember something.

What's wrong with me?

"Mom, it's so weird," I whisper. "It's so stupid. I can remember that I did drugs. I partied hard. I remember that, but nothing else really, since I pretty much died, like you all say. But now I'm here and I can't even walk or remember anything about anything. This totally feels like an actual nightmare."

The unexpected competency of putting thoughts into words propels the budding idea that this is not a dream. I have to pause for a long moment to gather my contemplations. Mom's rapt face prods me to continue my tirade.

"Waking up from dreams that I guess are actual dreams, and then being here, where it seems like I haven't actually woken up... it's crazy. It seems like I've just moved into another bad dream. I am always in a dream. Always."

Mom tightens her grip on my hand. Looking up at her, the tears trailing down her smiling face are so puzzling. How is it that people are almost always smiling or hopeful or positive around me when this whole so-called "real" life of mine is such a pathetic, nightmarish mess? Here Mom is, smiling while she cries on top of it.

"I love that you're talking to me." Her smile grows. "You were completely silent for almost a month. You're talking to me. It's beautiful." She closes her eyes, and with the most peaceful expression lifts her chin slightly. "You could say anything and I'd be overjoyed to hear it. But even when we couldn't hear you, there has always been one who could. One who has always been beside you, who snatched you from death's grip. Do you know who I mean, my girl?"

Mom's unexplainable peace in this tribulation should be a million-dollar question. Or it should be part of a dream.

Or it should be a divine intervention.

I've heard someone. But not really heard. More like felt. Not really felt, though, either. There's not a word for the experience, but there has definitely been *something* that has just been… deific. A whispered solace that could have been easily missed without the deafening silence that is my whole world.

"Mom… there is something… bigger. Something that is talking to me… I think. But it's not like some insane voice in my head. I'm pretty sure anyway. I think maybe God is around here."

With my last sentence, a stifled sob escapes Mom.

"Oh Amanda," she chokes, ever smiling. "Oh, Amanda." With closed eyes again, she lifts her face. "Thank you. Thank you, thank you."

I pull on her hand. "Mom, this garbage I remember, is it real?" Interrupting her rapturous state is easier than it should be. I need to know. "Was I there for Bailey before all this? Or," I squeeze my eyes closed, waiting for a slap to my heart, "was I a doped-up crackhead type of mom?"

Mom shakes her head and tousles my disgusting hair like I'm her little girl again. Her precious mothering never wavers, even to a physically and mentally repulsive adult daughter.

"You did some pretty scary things when you were a teenager. But that is all gone and forgotten. When Bailey was born, you were clean and sober. You are an amazing mom. You took care of your baby."

Sweet relief washes over me, quickly trailed by the slightest recall of moments surrounding my baby's birth. A vision of the hospital's maternity ward room arouses a feeling of being petrified to be in charge of a human life; even still, I was elated to be given the honour of holding her, looking at her, loving her, nurturing her. This tiny, magnificent person was my daughter. Somehow I know that I've never taken the divine privilege of raising my beloved Bailey lightly.

An enormous, relieved sigh quickly ejects me from my rumination with the biting chest pain that always goes with deep sighs. When my wincing expression brings slight alarm to Mom's face, I shake my head.

"I have to stop breathing," I offer with a snicker. "It stings."

She raises her eyebrows. "Not really that funny, Amanda."

I chuckle again. "I was kind of joking. Deep breaths are a little uncomfortable. Big sighs don't feel good at all though. It's fine. That'll go away, I'm pretty sure."

I don't want to talk about all the things physically wrong with me right now. Words are coming out of my mouth. Things are coming back to me. I have to get it all out before it goes away again.

"I just had another memory, I think," I continue, and Mom sits up eagerly. "At the hospital when Bailey was born. The feeling I had when I saw her. It was amazing, Mom."

Another tear escapes the corner of Mom's eye. "God has this whole thing. He has you. He is fixing you right back up. People have prayed hard, and God heard it all."

Such finality, such faith. My mother is a rock in this anarchy.

"Mom, I'm not trying to be stupid, but if this actually is a nightmare or hell or whatever, you are one of the only things that… lets me… hope, or something. Even though I have no choice, I really just couldn't do this without you."

Growing Up

PANTING, HEAD SPINNING, AND WITH ADRENALINE CRASHING THROUGH my body in waves from the top of my head to the tips of my toes, I waver somewhat before the words "find your centre" reverberate through me.

Sudden peals of laughter erupt from Lori, a couple of feet to my left. "Let's find you some dance shoes, woman! You owned this floor!"

I laugh too. It feels like I just ran a 5k race or something. What I just did was walk across the physio gym unassisted. Like an adult-sized toddler. Lori and Anne were within arm's reach the whole way, but I wasn't holding anything or being held by anyone. Being proud of myself for learning to walk is something straight out of a circus.

My wheelchair somehow appears behind me once I realize how much my legs are shaking in exhaustion. I grab two offered hands in front of me and lower myself into the chair. I glance up and see Anne beside Lori, and then I see that I'm still holding onto one of each of their hands. I blush and release my grip.

Anne's face becomes incredulous when she sees me blush. "Girl, I'm just going to assume you're all flushed because you just had a good work-out, not because you're embarrassed about anything. That was a giant leap for your recovery. Remember, you pretty much broke yourself in half and had a traumatic brain injury. Now you're walking on your own. Don't let me catch you blushing about anything except a bouquet from Kyle." She stares at me hard for a moment, then relaxes. "You got it, Amanda! Next step is, when you're a little more comfortable on your feet, we're going to see where your neck is at. Dr. Johnson told us you're going to have an MRI soon to check on your spine. If all is heading in the right direction, that CTO needs to come off in a couple of weeks. Now that we know you're more aware of yourself, the doctors think you should be able to handle yourself for short amounts of time without that plastic nuisance."

I know Lori has been watching me, but I can't stop my face's terror-driven paralysis. She reaches for my hand again and lays her other hand on my shoulder.

"What's scaring you, Amanda?" Lori asks gently.

I'm thinking too hard about my head rolling off my shoulders the moment the brace comes off. After a long pause, it occurs to me that it's my turn to talk.

"Um... I don't know. I can't imagine holding my head up. I don't know if I can. I know that's stupid. And my arm. It seems like I can feel it maybe a tiny bit more today, but wasn't the numbness because I took the brace off?"

I close my eyes. Did I just say that? I'm twenty-something. I'm learning how to walk. I'm worried about holding my head up on my own. What is wrong with me?

Bringing all my focus to my upper body, sheathed in the brace, I imagine the brace melting away. I catch my breath as I almost feel myself folding at the neck without the support I've come to depend on. This plastic apparatus quite literally holds my life.

"Amanda." Not a question. Lori wants me to look at her. So I do. "Don't think too hard about that right now. Just focus on walking. One thing at a time." She squeezes my hand like she often does. "You did have a spinal fracture. You broke your neck. You had brain trauma. You got hit by a semi, for goodness' sake. The very fact that you're even capable of learning to walk is incredible. Don't be hard on yourself. You should be so proud of yourself. What you're doing, even sitting there, looking at me and talking to me, is almost impossible. But you're doing all these things. You're walking. At first it looked like you might be paralyzed, yet here you are, walking. You can do anything. Absolutely anything. Do you understand?"

Déjà vu washes over me. Why do I feel like people are always saying the same things? Maybe they are. Either my stunned, infantile state gives them no choice but to repeat themselves incessantly or my brain damage is turning my mind into a skipping disc. Or both.

The idea of me staying in this state for the rest of my existence enters my constricted mind. If I have a soul inside this shell of myself, I imagine pieces of it being shredded off with every passing day.

Good grief. Whether I'm dreaming or not, dead or not, this has been going on for so long and might keep going on forever. I may as well try my best to make it a trace less unbearable.

"And the numbness, that was because you didn't realize the severity of your situation," Lori continues. "Who knows how you tossed your neck around while you were taking the brace off, and then attempting to walk on your own before you were ready? Your spine affects your whole body; the nerves connected to your spine go right down your arms. But now, the numbness is already wearing off, right? Your spine is probably stronger and more healed than we know."

"Ugh." I sit up straighter than the brace already forces me to. "Okay, so since I'm going to risk my head falling off my neck at some point, let's get started right now."

Lori raises an eyebrow, a slightly perplexed expression on her face. "Lady, you could get an Oscar for your theatrics. Fake it 'til you make it. You've got that down."

"Huh? Don't make me think too hard, Lori. I have brain damage, remember?" I attempt to wink, knowing my face could actually be doing anything; winking has never been a gift of mine.

Whoa. Winking has never been a gift of mine? Do I recall something about myself?

"Look at this girl, grinning like a clown," one of them jokes. "She's taking us all for a ride. She'll just get up, throw off her CTO, and moonwalk around us any minute now. An Oscar nominee, we have here."

So this is what it's like being human. Knowing something random, something completely irrelevant about myself, something that isn't painful to try to dig up in my foggy head. A casual memory. Is some part of me coming back to life?

"Kay, whatever. Let's just get this neck prison off," I mutter playfully, only half-joking. I wedge my fingers between my chin and the brace, shocked all over again at how constricting the device is.

A hand very quickly covers mine and gently pries my fingers off the CTO.

"Amanda, your enthusiasm is perfect. It's exactly what you need, but we need to make sure the timing is right," Anne says. "You need an MRI to see how your spine is healing. If we take the CTO off too early, it might spell disaster." She looks into my eyes, taking me down a notch with every word. "It will happen soon, I swear. I'm sure Dr. Johnson has your appointment made already. She told us this morning that she was going to schedule an MRI."

This rollercoaster is killing my will to keep on going. I start to yawn, but am immediately forced to stifle it when my jaw refuses to open past a certain, very small angle. Wincing in pain, my hands fly to my face to provide some relief. At the same time, I feel like I remember someone saying something about TMJ, some kind of jaw situation caused by the impact and aggravated by the neck brace. I have no idea what that is, or if someone actually said it to me. But the idea of remembering some other small fact elates me, even amid this frustration.

"This is insane. My head is all over the place," I whine, trying to sound less disgruntled than I feel. Awkwardly, I stifle another yawn. "Can I go to bed?"

"Definitely. You've earned some beauty sleep."

Reformatory

"I'm going to hold up these flashcards; you're going to tell me what picture is on the card. Simple as that." Miriam points to the stack in her other hand. "These photos are different everyday things. Nothing too crazy."

She clears her throat as she shuffles the pile as if it's a deck of playing cards.

I have to stifle the twitch that's burning my eye. It's a mystery how Miriam has been one of the banes of my Riverview existence, especially since I can't even really recall any of my encounters with this speech therapist. Whatever my beef with her is, though, it's enough to make me dread the very thought of speech therapy.

I clear my own throat and smile. "Okay, go ahead."

Miriam meets my eyes before lifting the first card. I once again suppress that twitch. I blink very slowly and deliberately. My eyes open to a photo of a little fur ball.

After a beat, I say, "kitten."

Another photo. Another beat.

"Sh... shovel."

Another photo.

"Uh, pen."

Another, but this time I pause for a longer moment.

"Book... map. Map book? I know that's not the word."

With an unmoving expression, Miriam chirps, "Atlas, my dear."

"Ah shoot, I knew that."

"What's this one?"

"Uh... restaurant... guy."

"Chef, Amanda."

"Oh."

Another photo.

"Uh, um… pa… path."

"Street, actually," she sings, peering over her glasses.

She holds up another card. I stare at it until my focus feels like it's breaking though the surface. I know what the picture is, but nothing comes to me. Not a word. I shake my head and drop my gaze to the floor.

"Football, Amanda."

Why does she seem so smug? I'm trying.

"Hey now, don't be discouraged. Your mind will get around all these roadblocks soon enough. You need to keep trying."

Swallowing hard, I leave my eyes on the ground for a few seconds as a response swirls through my head. This woman, what is my issue with her?

Brief flashes of past speech sessions drop into my consciousness. In them, I'm faltering over words, letters, and sounds.

"Amanda, slow down. Think about the words before you say them."

"That's not exactly right, Amanda. Try it this way instead."

"Amanda, slow down."

"Amanda, don't think so hard about it. Just say what's on your mind."

"Ugh," I blurt, covering my face. "I can't talk. My brain has nothing."

Maybe it's not Miriam I can't stand. Maybe it's just talking. Maybe it's just my messed up head.

No, Miriam isn't being cool about this, either. She's so nitpicky. She doesn't smile unless I make some kind of mistake, which I do all the time. She doesn't ever smile *at me.*

And then there's the speech room, a small space that makes me feel like the walls are closing in on me. The room is a little box, with only one tiny window in some corner that no one could easily look out of. The walls are brown; it might be an attempt at light brown, maybe a haphazard shot at lightening the mood, but it looks more like a sickly form of bodily waste. Miriam always closes the door behind us, so the room is deafeningly silent unless someone's speaking; when there are words, they're always clipped, to-the-point, no-nonsense words.

This room is killing me. I need to get out of here.

"I'm just going to go to the bathroom for a minute," I mumble without looking at Miriam.

"Amanda, this stuff needs all of your focus."

Am I with at a drill sergeant or a speech therapist?

"Be sure you're not interrupting yourself unnecessarily."

What does that even mean? Not that I really care. I'm more concentrated on the fact that right now I have the knowledge to compare her to a drill sergeant. It doesn't excite me to be able to compare her to something so uncool, but the fact that I'm able to do it without even really... well, it must mean something.

"It's fine. I need to pee." I try to make it come out light-hearted, but I wonder if I sound as annoyed as I truly feel. Miriam stares through me with an irritated countenance. Just as quickly as I think of covering up my annoyance, the thought is replaced by the urge to defend my mood.

"Will you need some assistance to get to the washroom, dear?" Miriam asks. "I can call for someone."

There's a bathroom one door down from the speech room and I'm confident it won't be an issue to get there. With a burdensome breath, I grab my chair's armrests tightly, then lean back and push myself forward to stand.

"I'm good, thanks." I hope the assertive tone will silence her.

Holding onto the top of the chair's backrest, I turn and face the door. Feeling Miriam's gaze pierce my back drives me to get out of here even more. I stride toward the door in the most natural-feeling gait I've had yet. I open the door and step out into the hall and carry on to the bathroom, just like any other person.

Confidence. This is winning. Although I'm faking it, to a degree, it puts some wind in my sails.

Geez. Getting annoyed and walking away from something, comparing someone to a drill sergeant... what does it mean that I'm so motivated by these incredibly thoughtless things?

The bathroom greets me more brightly than the speech room with its white walls and tripled size. I make a beeline for the closest stall; I need to sit down before I get too carried away with my newfound walking freedom and bite the linoleum.

Standing up from the toilet, pausing to wash my hands, and then moving back to the speech room is so much harder than leaving the forsaken chamber. I can't decide what's harder: returning to the room or the acts of sitting, standing, and walking again. Either way, my upper lip is beaded with sweat by the time I return to the hostage chair.

Miriam's absence behind her desk halts me. I shuffle my body into a position that allows me to read the name on the outside of the door: *Speech Therapy, Miriam Dickins*.

I guess I didn't return to the wrong room. Hopefully she doesn't come back.

I hope she comes back right now, actually. It's so quiet in here. There's not another person around, for all I can hear. Maybe this is the part of my nightmare where it actually becomes hell and I'm left alone in desolation for the rest of my existence.

The seconds each feel like an hour. I can't hear anybody.

The thing that I've been terrified of is finally happening. I don't remember anything, really. I have no prior life. All I can think of is empty, never-ending halls in Riverview, a tiny hellhole for speech, and my own obnoxious room. I'd rather be shuddering in my bed than in this condemning speech room. My trembling has gotten so severe that my neck aches more deeply.

I clench my eyelids and examine the blank slate of my memory for anything: people, places, the most mundane occurrences, life. The dark hole of Riverview swallows the slate whole. This place is my entire reality. Yet it's so unreal that there's no possible way it could be anything but hell. Even behind closed eyes, the blackness spirals in a dizzying array.

Feeling wetness trickle down my cheek tells me that this can't be a nightmare. I wouldn't feel the tears on my face if this were a dream.

The reeling in my head grows to a sickening height before it's stopped violently by the sight of a monstrous semi within arm's reach and getting closer by every fraction of a second. So fast that it takes my breath away, the truck is replaced with blackness of every colour.

"Amanda." A voice slices through the dark. Sterile-looking tiles on the floor come into view. The biting pain in the palms of my hands tells me my fists were clenched hard, my long fingernails coiled inside them.

"Amanda," someone says again. "Is everything all right?"

My sight lifts to find Miriam standing in front of me, examining me with her meticulous gawk.

"Uh… yeah… thanks," I push past the lump in my throat, managing to sound so much more nonchalant than I feel. Miriam continues to inspect me as she backs into her chair. She meets my gaze for uncomfortably long moments, but I hold her gaze until she looks away.

I can't tell this woman my heart. Or head-trip, or whatever that just was. Did I just see my accident? I feel myself come apart with each passing second, even while I'm trying, with everything I have, to appear unchanged. I can't tell this lady anything. She doesn't seem human.

I stumble through the rest of the session on autopilot. Miriam often looks me over, pausing on my face, pumping me for information.

After an eternity, Miriam rises from her chair and gives me another once-over.

"We're done for today, Amanda," she says, pulling open the door. "Kyle is here to help you back up to your room. Have a good afternoon."

With these parting words, she nods at Kyle just outside the doorway and moves past him.

I let out a relieved huff of air with the grin that cracks my stony face. It feels like I was holding my breath the whole hour. Before we even started, I was waiting to be finished.

Knowing I can finally leave this horrible room, standing up is the easiest it's ever been. I get up fast enough to leave Kyle gaping at me.

"Uh, what's up? Besides you?" he questions with his brows raised.

I can tell him when I'm sitting down. I'm a clown when it comes to walking and talking at the same time. I grip his offered arm and almost pull him forward in my impatience to leave this part of Riverview behind and escape with one of my few existing hopes.

Kyle walks me to the elevator, and up to my room's floor we go. The silence is killing him; I feel him looking at me intently. Actually, it's probably my ease of standing up and bolting ahead of him that has him at a loss for words.

When I finally and exhaustedly stumble through my room's doorway, I let another huff of air escape and continue to my bed. I drop to the pillow without even looking around the room.

Kyle clears his throat a little too hard.

"What?"

"You have company," he says. "You can ignore me if you want, but I know you don't want your other visitor to leave without saying hi." I push myself up to see who I'm hosting. "Don't think you can just not talk, though. What was that, exactly?"

When my searching eyes finally land on Chelsea, my mouth explodes into a smile that actually hurts.

"Chelsea ... Chelsea." I can't get anything past my lips except the name of my beautiful visitor.

Chelsea beams back at me as she jumps to her feet and grabs both of my hands.

"Hi babe," she says in her calm voice. I recognize it as fast as her matchless face. Just as calmly, as if she's talking about the weather, she continues, "Get better and get your butt home. I miss you so much. You scared the life out of me."

My mind is spinning. I can't find a word to vocalize except her name. I can't believe I know someone. Then another person occurs to me: a tiny, curly-haired boy, Chelsea's son, around the same age as Bailey. My baby girl who is not here. Someone else is taking care of her, someone who is not her mommy.

Wetness trails down the sides of my face before I grasp that I look like an idiot in front of my dear friend who I don't really remember, but I know. All I've said to her is her name, and then I started sobbing.

Wow.

"Sorry," I mutter, reaching for a tissue on the bedside table; Chelsea holds the box up in front of me before my hand gets too far. I guess brain-damaged people are predictable. I chuckle stupidly before looking up at my friend and my fiancé, both eyeing me in confused awe.

Mocking a confession, I raise one hand.

"Brain damage." A sneer splits my face. "So that means I'm going to suck at talking and not crying and stuff. Is that cool?"

After an awkward pause, Kyle and Chelsea both snicker. I join in quickly. Laughter tightens my lungs and makes me hesitate to keep going, but the ridiculousness of not being able to laugh and the absurd state I'm in leave me no choice but to laugh even harder. Despite my chest tightening painfully, the fog over my heart lifts and pacifies the sting.

Kyle and Chelsea both eye me approvingly. I'm guessing they like to see my face doing something other than crying, sleeping, or looking completely stunned.

"So, pretty much what happened is, when I was in speech, I had a dream or something. But I was awake, so it wasn't a dream. It was so weird. Whatever it was, I saw the truck that hit me. Like, right before it hit me. Like a second before."

I stop, almost breathless from saying so much, so fast. Does that even make any sense? It occurs to me that going from just saying her name a few times to having some kind of epiphany is probably not the most social thing to do.

"Oh, sorry, Chels. Hi! I'm so glad you came. I'm sorry, I probably look pretty gross. I hope you weren't expecting to see me looking normal." The mess of words comes out so fast. She most likely can't even understand me.

Her hand falls on top of mine again. "Babe, I have been here to see you since the first day they let me in. Even at the hospital. You're looking like a million bucks. You're not six feet under. You couldn't be more beautiful."

She has seen me like this? I don't even know what I look like, but I know it can't be good. My hair feels like a greasy rat's nest, I'm missing a couple of front teeth, and the rest of me is covered in plastic. Sick.

"Uh, Amanda, do you remember what you just said to me?" Kyle jumps in, sounding agitated. "Did you really see that?"

My mind jumps back to the disturbing image of thousands of pounds of metal flying at me. Then nothing. But also, everything at once.

"Amanda."

The sound of my name pulls me from a disturbed trance. "What?"

"You told me you saw the semi. For real?" Kyle asks again, pacing slowly beside my bed.

"Uh, yeah. Only for a second. But the second doesn't end. There's a lot of black after. Or before, I don't know." I stumble through my words, throwing out whatever surfaces.

"I'm going to tell Wade," he says. "Maybe you're remembering something crazy."

Kyle drops my hand and moves toward the door. His swift exit would normally be devastating, but Chelsea's presence balms the wound. Her face is serene. Reassuring. Nothing can faze this girl.

A slideshow of moments with Chelsea runs through my head. No particular events, just instances in time with my dear friend. There's no indication of anything but a comfortable familiarity between us.

Suddenly, among those images is one of her feisty little guy sitting beside my Bailey. Jaxon. His name is Jaxon.

"What are you looking so amused about all of a sudden?" she asks with a chuckle.

"Jaxon. I remember Jaxon. That's your boy." I know this. I don't need to ask her. Who knew that the ability to remember facts of life would be such an exhilarating thing?

Chelsea whoops. "Yes!"

"There's a party up in here!" Wade howls as he strolls into the room with Kyle.

"This girl just remembered my son without me even mentioning him," Chelsea says in her cool voice, her face radiating the elation I feel.

Wade turns his head to me with his brows raised halfway up his forehead. "Look at you, Amanda. Remembering people, remembering the semi. Seems like you might have some stories to tell us."

Intrigue exudes from all the faces in front of me. Weird. Just recalling stuff is huge in this crazy place.

"Uh, well, just for like a second I saw a huge truck, pretty much right in my mouth. It was so close. But that was it." I stop and gasp with an abrupt, awful thought. "Does that mean I could have stopped if I saw it? But I didn't?"

"It's a flashback. Nothing more, nothing less," Wade jumps in. "We know you tried to stop, because you braked so hard that your vehicle's tires laid some serious rubber into the highway. You probably won't remember anything else about your accident because you were unconscious right away, for a couple of weeks. Thank God for that, because you wouldn't want to remember anything else about it. But this is incredible, girl. Your memory is coming back. You're on the road to recovery, and now you're in the fast lane. Walking like a champ, mostly independent with everyday functions, and amusing the heck out of everyone all the time."

"Whoa, wait. What's amusing about my gimpy-ness?" I joke.

"Hey, not gimpy-ness. None of that. I just meant your magic recovery has everyone amused."

"Nothing magic about it Wade," I boast. "There's really only one way this could have happened."

I stop and cross my arms with smug countenance. Wade just looks at me expectantly, waiting for me to go on. When I don't keep talking, he crosses his arm, leans back on his heels, and looks around the room casually as if he has all the time in the world.

Pretending to sigh in exasperation, I speak. "God, obviously. There's no other way. God. Only God."

Suddenly, I'm swayed by the thought that I have no idea where Wade stands with his belief in an all-powerful Creator. Hoping I haven't offended or weirded him out, my eyes drop from his face to my hands.

"And, like, you guys here at this place are here for me because God knew you were what I needed," I quickly add. "You are all amazing. I couldn't do this without you people. All of you."

I fiddle with my blanket, twisting and bunching it. It might have been better when I wasn't able to talk so easily.

"Hey, that's cool," Wade says. "I'm sure your prayers, and everyone else's, help you out."

I feel slight relief, tampered with misunderstanding. I have no idea what that means about how he was affected by what I said, or if it affected him at all. Maybe he agrees. Maybe he doesn't. Maybe he's unsure. Whatever his thoughts are, I wonder what his story is.

The sound of Wade's footsteps as he leaves the room brings me back to Kyle and my precious friend. I grin at them and open my arms, waiting for someone to come hug me. When people are with me, it feels as if no time passes—until they leave again. I've got to soak up the time they give me.

A thrilling idea pops into my head when Chelsea swoops in for a hug.

"Hey, do you think they'd let us go outside?" I squeak, anticipation coursing through all of me. "I know I'm not good at walking and stuff, but do you think they'd let you guys take me out in my wheelchair? They'd have to know that you wouldn't let me leave."

Kyle and Chelsea exchange glances that quickly become more relaxed, even excited, when they realize I'm not trying to get them to break me out. I'll be devastated if it isn't allowed to happen.

"Please, please?" I ask. "The walls of this place are eating me alive. Please?"

"Well, I'll go talk to Wade, but I think that should be cool." Kyle starts to leave, then pauses for a second. He grunts, more to himself than to us. "Actually, I don't need to ask. I'll just go tell him where we're going."

His words are music to my ears.

Stunning, noisy, multifaceted. The world, so welcome, comes into focus as my beloved pushes my wheelchair out the front doors of my penitentiary. Chelsea walks beside me. I hear wind in the trees, birds, cars… so many more reverberations I can't and don't even care to identify. I'm entranced by the commotion. This is what life sounds like, not the deathly silence that lies behind the doors I just escaped.

There's no one thing I can rest my eyes on for more than a second. My gaze darts from one fascinating piece of life to another. As Kyle pushes me along a path that extends toward a large fountain, the slideshow of images stops on a memory of a house I know I've lived in. Another flick, and I see the field behind my old high school, slowly replaced by the parking lot of a building I worked inside at some point. My next apparition is the expanse of the backyard of my daughter's daycare. Reality looms large; I'm seeing the place that's replacing me as mommy.

Before I can bawl, the daycare image is exchanged for the inside of a car I don't know, but I recognize. I hear a male voice that I don't know, but I recognize. A feeling of betrayal and guilt I recognize, but can't identify. Then the face of a man I recognize, but can't place the extent or purpose of the encounter; I only discern the heavy mood. I know it's not right. I can't distinguish anything about what's happening in the still frames of my mind, except that it's not right.

A hand on my arm and the forced, weighty release of air from my lungs pulls me out of the eerie memories. My eyelids blink away the haze blanketing my awareness. Stifling the tremors that would take over my body if I thought any more about this weird mind game, I bring the world in front of me into focus and push everything else out.

"Wow," I gasp, equally exhausted by and in awe of my surroundings. My people, standing on either side of me in front of the fountain, both put a hand on my shoulders.

My people. Whatever life was before, whoever was in it, none of it could involve anyone more important than my people. The ones who I hold in my memory now, as sparse as it may be, are the only ones who could have meant anything of importance to me—the ones who have been here, and the others who still might come.

Whatever mess is shading my newfound memory just now, that familiar but unknown man obviously isn't one of my people. Therefore, he doesn't matter. I don't need to finish that memory. I won't.

I switch my attention to the beautiful shots of my life, the true memories of places I once knew. Memories. Painful acknowledgments of real life made breathtaking by my alien ability to recall them.

Content with the new, old, real scenes playing across my heart, my hands lift and cover the ones resting on my shoulders.

Whatever is happening to me, I am loved by someone.

First responders searching for any sign of life in the wreckage.

The best face of my vehicle after it was flattened.

Emergency crews working tirelessly to stabilize me.

One of many Godsends, STARS air ambulance, descending to carry me
across flooded highways and to the hospital as quickly as possible.

So many different responders working together to save my life.

Fall from Grace

THE MALE VOICE THAT SO PROFOUNDLY DISTURBED ME YESTERDAY shakes me awake. I'm lying here, dazed. Hours pass. Mental pictures of the man's face break into my life story. I don't know where it belongs, though. I have no timeframe for it, or anything else for that matter. I just know that the encounter isn't what it should have been. That's all I know, which is enough to squeeze my heart, hard.

I know this person isn't someone of importance to me. I can perceive enough about him to know he won't come visit me, because my impressions of him carry so much guilt. Extreme guilt. It courses through me with every turn my mind makes in that direction. The conviction that comes along with it confuses and enrages me.

What could possibly have happened?

"Ugh," I growl, so much louder than I intended. I kick my legs, restless, until they end up twisted in the sheets. Annoyed, I break a sweat working to unravel them without sitting up. When I finally succeed, my ensuing roll onto my side takes a lot longer than it should, annoying me further still.

"Amanda, what's going on?" someone asks, peeking around the door. It's the night nurse, another one whose face I know, but I don't feel like I've seen before.

With beads of sweat running into my eyes, I swat at the bedside table in search of a tissue to wipe the moisture off my forehead. The nurse scurries over to help. At the urgency in her walk, I guess I must look like more of a wreck than I usually do. When she frowns, confused at my morbid chuckle, I know I need to help her out.

"Don't worry, I'm not dying or anything," I say. "I just can't sleep."

"Have you been awake for long?"

"A long time. I can't sleep."

"How long would you say you've been up? Were you able to fall asleep at all tonight?"

I know I fell asleep, because I remember waking up. Still, it doesn't feel like I've slept at all, so I have no idea how to begin to answer her question. Do I tell her I'm having nightmares of some craziness that I know happened but can't even identify? No way; I don't need to sound crazier than I already am.

"I might have fallen asleep at the beginning. I don't know. I think I did. But I've been awake for most of the night, I think."

She writes something on a small notepad she pulls out of the front pocket of her scrubs. "Maybe we can't lower the dose yet."

I've been taking tiny white cups full of crushed pills for as long as I can remember. I assume she's talking about one of those powdered piles I've been choking down.

"I'll be right back," she says. "We're going to need to top up your sleep aid, my dear."

She spins on her heel and exits the room.

The thought of dumping another pile of dust onto my tongue distracts me enough to forget why I'm awake in the first place. Suppressing a gag, I reach for the cup of thickened water on my bedside table and sip at it to clear my throat and brace myself for the oncoming repulsion. The denseness of the drink doesn't help. How have I been drinking this garbage?

When the nurse returns, she sees me working my mouth in a show of disgust after my drink of jellylike water. She actually smiles when I look at her. Is she enjoying how gross this is to me?

"Oh, Amanda, you know what this means?" At my blank stare, she continues quickly. "I can see how disgusted you are by that water, which we haven't seen in you yet. You might be ready for normal water again."

I haven't even thought about why I'm drinking this joke of a beverage. Now I need to know what they're doing to me.

"Why? Why do I need this gross stuff?" I ask, trying not to let my aggravation be heard in my voice.

"It was only to keep you safe. Thick fluids are a lot less likely to get into your lungs; you had some very serious respiratory issues. You've also had to relearn to swallow, and thickened drinks aren't as easy to choke on."

I can see that there's only sincerity in this nurse. These people at Riverview all seem to be pretty sweet. Except for the speech therapist. Well, she's not that bad, I guess, but all I remember about speech is that I'm always uncomfortable there. Maybe this isn't just a nightmare. Maybe this is really where I am, thickened water and all.

I take the offered cup with the crushed pill, pause, and try to throw up some kind of mental block to swallowing a mound of grime. I dump it into my mouth and immediately chase it with the excuse for water. My block doesn't work, and I gag hard once it's down my throat. Ignoring the revulsion washing over me is easy when taken with the heightened pain in my neck from the sudden gagging motion. I smother my blanket into my face to keep from screaming in frustration.

The nurse places her hand on my back, stopping me. I quickly pull the blanket from my face, embarrassed at my incompetence and weakness.

"I'll just try to go sleep. Sorry." I don't know what else to say.

I lower myself down to the pillow. The nurse looks down at me for a minute, adjusts my blanket like a mom, then slowly backs out of the room.

Left alone with my insanity, I have nothing to do but close my eyes and try to let sleep overtake me.

I'm driving down the highway, east toward the town my parents live in. I'm running away from that face, hiding from that face. Hiding from so many people. No one can see this. No one.

See what?

The highway to my parents' hometown goes on. And on and on. The lights of the town on the evening's horizon are within sight. So close, I could touch them. So far away, I can't reach them.

Time without beginning or end passes. I perpetually drive toward the lights. They never grow brighter or larger; they stay just as they are. Beyond my reach. Forever beyond my reach.

The squeeze of my empty lungs evokes a gasp for precious oxygen, throwing me into consciousness. Blinking furiously, I fight to bring my surroundings into focus. I need to be anywhere but where I just was. I don't know where I was, or what was happening; I just need to be anywhere else.

The cold, hard plastic of my glasses being slid onto my face shocks me for a moment before I realize someone is trying to put them on for me. I close my eyes tightly, then open them to see who's with me.

My rigid face breaks into a teary smile when I see Mom, Dad, and her: my little girl. My parents and my Bailey.

I have no idea what to do. I don't need to do anything. I just need to stare at my baby and my parents. Examining every inch of my sweet daughter, trying to lock her image in my heart and at the front of my mind, my vision becomes blurred by tears.

When my dad whispers something to Bailey, my contemplation moves to him. Daddy. Studying his face brings to mind instances of his life, being my dad, being rock-solid.

"Daddy," I whisper, reaching for his hand.

He shuffles quickly to my side and grabs both of my hands. Using his hands for leverage, I pull myself up to sit—and then keep pulling. I need my daddy to hold me. I need his strong arms around me.

He carefully enfolds me in the softest and most secure dad-hug. Neither of us let go for a long time. I know that he's a trucker, that he's not always around, and I know I need to cherish any time I have with him. Until right now, this hasn't even occurred to me.

The thought of my idiocy crosses my mind, but it feels kind of impressed on me that this memory should just be celebrated for what it is: a memory. I don't have many of those.

With Dad so close, Mom seems to sense that now is a good time for my baby, to whom I'm almost a stranger, to be brought close. Mom sits Bailey beside me on my bed, where she's still within arm's reach of my dad.

It is not lost on me that my own baby doesn't know me anymore. She's scared of me. Which makes sense; I look like a freak of nature, and I've been away from her for forever. I have no idea how long exactly, but I know it's been way too long.

"Bailey. Hi monkey." I force myself to speak lightly, knowing that a lot of emotion will probably freak her out.

Dad lets go, but doesn't move away too fast. Instead, he moves to eye level with my girl, who has started to whimper. He grins into her exquisite little face and taps her on the nose.

"Your momma is right here, Bailey," he coaxes, motioning toward me. "Can you say hi to her? I am right here beside you."

Bailey swats at my dad's glasses, pushed up on the top of his head. She giggles when he catches her hand and tickles her armpit.

"Papa," she squeaks captivatingly, snickering. She snorts.

I feel my face erupt into an easy grin, a beautifully familiar, too-long-absent sense of being Mommy to this sweet girl. I could listen to her endearing laugh forever.

I want to hold her more than anything. Knowing that it's probably not possible right now, for a million reasons, I reach my hand toward her and just let it stay there, waiting for anything. A swat, a grab, a high-five, anything. I need contact with my child. My heart burns with a mixture of joy, misery, desperation, and hope.

Bailey's eyes slowly trail up my arm to my face. Finally, her eyes reach mine. Recognition and hesitation flicker across her face. It seems like she wants to reach out to my hand.

"Papa," she says as she throws an arm up, reaching for him.

Dad takes her hand but doesn't pick her up.

"Papa," she says again as she drops her other hand of top of Dad's and pats it a few times, smiling. Observing everything about her, I can count at least five teeth along her gums. I'm exhilarated by the new/old knowledge that she was a late teether who didn't even have any teeth by her first birthday. A strange sense bubbles up my throat that can only be released in laughter.

Watching my daughter in merriment like this, being so close to her, and having Mom and Dad with me, feels home-like. They feel so recent, even more… current… than Kyle. I can't organize in my mind exactly what I'm feeling, but it just feels like there's more to this than what's right before my eyes.

"Mom, Dad… why does this feel like it just barely happened or something? I mean, we probably visited you a lot, because you're Grandma and Grandpa and my parents, but it just feels like I lived with you right before this or something. But obviously I lived with Kyle. Where did we live? What exactly was happening? I can't figure anything out. What was going on?"

Mom and Dad exchange weighty glances, as if they don't know what exactly to say. Mom picks up Bailey, who's straining to reach for someone other than me, and seats herself on the bedside chair. She runs her fingers through Bailey's soft, wispy hair, pondering something deeply.

What does this mean? I just asked where I lived, or something to that effect. I'm not even really sure what I asked, and now the air is so thick I could roll right out of this ridiculous place on top of it.

"Well," Mom finally begins, "you might not have been in the best place with your family life right when this happened. Or you might have been in a great place; it was really hard to tell."

She stops and wrinkles her brow, searching for what to say next.

"With an explanation like that, I'm just going to shut up, sit here, and not move until you tell me the whole story," I mutter, irritated by her beating around the bush.

"You asked for it, so here it goes, I guess. Remember, I'm not judging you, just telling you." Mom passes Bailey off to Dad. She returns to the chair and folds her hands in her lap. "You, Kyle, and Bailey lived in Niverville. Kyle worked in Winnipeg, for a really big company that has locations all over the place. He was transferred to Alberta, so all three of you packed up and moved to Alberta. When you got there, you didn't love it, and after a couple of months you were desperate to come back.

"After being away from God for many years, you were also working at getting closer to him. You found a church out there which you went to without Kyle because you said he wasn't too interested in it. You told us you had made a close friend at church, and also had met with the pastor a few times. When you called us, you didn't go into a lot of detail about it, but you eventually said you just felt it pressed on you to move back out here and not live with Kyle until you were married because you needed to start again with you purity and dedication to God."

She stops short and shakes her head. Furrowing her brow at me, she scooches forward on her chair and grabs my hands.

"Do you want me to stop? I don't want to upset you. I'm not sure how much I should put into your head right now."

Equally intrigued to hear that I actually existed before, and filled with trepidation to hear more about what I used to be, I'm at a loss for words. Obviously it's not good; my mother doesn't even want to tell me about myself. I need to know, though. I need to understand what my heart and head are at war over.

Nodding as furiously as my stunted spine and rigid brace will allow seems to communicate to Mom that she needs to keep talking. She looks at Dad questioningly, and my patience is instantly snapped by the realization that people are hesitating to fill me in on my own circumstances.

"Tell me everything you know," I say. "Tell me why I'm here. Well, I know, kind of, but tell me exactly what led up to this. This can't just be some freak accident. There has to be a reason. Or something. Tell me how this happened."

I stop myself from carrying on and boiling up to an eruption, even with my intense craving to agonize, loudly, over every painstaking second of the shards of life I can remember.

"Please," I add softly, imploringly.

Mom, in an extraordinary show of love, strength, resignation, and parental correction, just nods and starts in on her account of her wayward daughter's final moments again.

"We were pretty hesitant about just taking you and Bailey back in and leaving Kyle two provinces away without his fiancé and daughter, but at the same time we were excited that you were looking to renew your relationship with Christ. Since Kyle was only intending on staying in Alberta for less than a year and then transfer back to Manitoba, Dad and I agreed to have you and Bailey move back home until you and Kyle got married. So, when Kyle had a couple of weeks off for Christmas holidays, you guys came back to visit, but Kyle left you and Bailey here and went back to Alberta. It was obvious that it was killing him, but he just wanted you to be happy."

Mom pauses to sip at her coffee as she wrinkles her brow, looking like she's unsure of what to say next. A squeal of laughter from Bailey seems to shake some words into Mom, and she continues.

"When you got home, you were so happy and radiant about starting over and being where you felt like you belonged. It didn't take long, though, before you seemed like you were fading off into your own world again. You'd take Bailey and go to visit old friends, but it seemed like maybe those old friends were sounding boards for you, and you would just tell them how you felt so unrestful with Kyle and everything else. Every time you came home you seemed a little more set on starting over in every way, whether that included Kyle or not. You were so agitated about something.

"Then, well," Mom blows out a puff of air as if she's about to get into the brunt of something, "one day I noticed you weren't wearing your engagement ring, and then the next day, the same thing. You kept on not wearing it, and it became clear you hadn't just forgotten it. When I'd ask you about it, you always said you forgot, or changed the subject. All of a sudden, you stopped saying anything, just giving me a look that said you were done wearing it at all. When Kyle was transferred back home from Alberta at the end of May, you put your ring back on when you two saw each other, but even that ended after a few visits.

"Before I could finally sit you down and talk to you for real, you and Sheri had plans one evening, and you were about to be off again. When you asked me last minute if I would mind keeping Bailey for you, I told you I was busy and wouldn't be able to that night. So you started getting her ready to go with you, but for some reason, which I now understand as God nudging me, I told you I had changed my plans and would babysit Bailey."

She's suddenly coughing softly with a tissue to her eyes, trying to smother her tears. When those tears only become heavier and her shoulders start shaking, she finally gives in and speaks through the whimpers.

"Well, that's all I can tell you about where you were at. You didn't tell me anything specific about what was happening with you, or between you and Kyle."

Dazed by the familiar strangeness of her tale, it takes me a minute to connect her story's ending of me leaving Bailey with her before...

"Mom, what's wrong? What happened next?" I ask, despite knowing the answer. Closing my eyes, I wait for the impact.

She clears her throat a couple of times, and then plunges into the end.

"About half an hour after you planned to meet Sheri, she called to see if you were on your way. I told her you had left an hour ago. It only takes about half an hour to get to her house from ours. We both tried calling you right away; even though we knew thirty minutes isn't all that late, you were always a very punctual person and it just didn't feel right that you weren't there yet." Her speech gets more halted and tense as she delves further into the tale. "You didn't show up. Finally, Kenny went out to see if he could find your vehicle.

"Once he got onto the highway, it didn't take him long to see the sirens. There your SUV was, wedged under the trailer of a semi, flat as a pancake." With the kind of strength only my mother has, she carries on. "You were airlifted to Winnipeg. Which was another miracle. STARS air ambulance was in the province that spring because there was a lot of flooding all over, and emergencies would have taken way too long to respond to without them here." Mom smiles shakily toward the ceiling. "You wouldn't have made it if a ground ambulance had to go through all the detours to get you to the hospital.

"When we got to the hospital, they couldn't tell us what was happening with you. We could only wait. Jesus waited with us.

"I wasn't even aware of time anymore; it just felt like an eternity. At some point, we were told that you had cervical spine fractures, brain trauma, punctured lungs, broken ribs, and so many other things. For days, they just kept telling us you might not make it through the day, then they'd tell us you might not make it through the night.

"Through all of it, there were a mass people praying. And God listened. He gave me this peace that shouldn't have existed." Mom stops again, but this time her face is radiant with wonder. "You're here now. You're talking to us, you're moving, you're awake. You're alive."

The spinning details in my mind are a fiery hurricane of emotion. In the eye of the storm, though, there is peace. There was the strongest, most secure safeguard around Bailey. My daughter was under God's wing. There is no doubt in my heart that He was the only reason Mom changed her mind. Even after the account of how this all went down, I feel so content in the knowledge that before I faced my biggest downfall, there was a hand in the midst of it all to shield the beat of my heart.

"Girl, you have every reason to be laughing," Dad says, bewilderment on his face. "Death has no power where God is. I have to know, though, why are you laughing all of a sudden?"

I inhale sharply to catch my breath. How do people laugh and talk at the same time? I didn't even realize I was laughing, but it feels so good. What else can I do when I'm so deep in such a weird set of circumstances?

"Well, geez, my vehicle was crushed flat as a pancake, apparently," I say. "I pretty much died. Bailey would have been with me, except for some random change in Mom's mind. Bailey is safe and happy, but if Mom had kept her plans, Bailey would not be okay. And now I'm not dying. Not even close, it seems like. What else can I do but laugh?"

Dad chuckles softly. "I see your point."

"Mama," Bailey squeals. My head whips in her direction faster than has ever been possible before, and my ensuing scream is smothered when I jam my fist into my mouth. It comes out in a strangled growl.

"Mama, mama," Bailey chirps again.

In spite of the waves of agony coursing through my neck, I blink away the tears flooding my eyes and behold my girl. I can't believe she's calling me her mama. This elation could balm anything.

"Mama, mama."

My baby, my girl, is gazing at my mom with rapt attention, love and adoration inscribed all over her sweet face. Mom is not smiling. She's pointing at me with each of Bailey's words.

"Grandma. Nana. I am nana," Mom says gently, but firmly. "Your mama is right here." She points immovably at me, while Bailey pulls at her arm.

The colour drains from my face and my hope withers. This opens the floodgates of my heart, and bitter tears streams down my face. I can't stop myself. There's no point anyway. My baby is no longer my baby. She doesn't know me anymore.

"Bailey, my little... monkey," I choke out between sobs. "Remember? My... monkey."

Bailey gapes at me, still pulling at Mom's arm. The wheels are turning in her head. She seems to know there's more to me than just some sideshow freak covered in plastic, but she doesn't think I'm Mama.

Lifting her delicate little finger and pointing it at me, she says softly, "Mama?"

My solemnity breaks as fast as it set in, and I feel myself beaming at her. I can't instantly push any words around my fragile hope. I swallow hard a few times before my mouth can form any words. I take a shaky breath.

"Yes, monkey, it's me. Mama. I love you forever, baby girl. I love you so much. I'm coming home to you as soon as I can. I love you."

My tone is edged with pleading. Although I hear it and try in earnest to squeeze it out of my voice, it doesn't go away. This girl is my life. The empty abyss of my mind still knows the beat of my heart.

Bailey tilts her head at me and studies my face in a charming examination. I'd give anything to scoop her into my arms and kiss her sweet face. Trapped in a twilight zone, knowing my existence is fully indefinite by the flesh of my flesh, I can't move. I'm paralyzed, waiting for acknowledgment.

"Mama," she says with certainty.

My eyes widen, and it sounds like someone cheers in the background. My head feels suddenly numb. The magic of her statement must have been imagined in my desperation. Can't be real.

"Mama," she says again, more forcefully.

Is she talking to my mom? She lifts her finger again and stabs the air in my direction.

"Mama!" she says once more, sounding agitated.

Whoa. I think I'm hearing her right.

My mom hops up with Bailey's declaration and practically jumps to my bedside with Bailey in her arms.

"Do you want to go to mama?" she asks, inching Bailey down beside me.

"No. No. Nana, no." She twists away from me and pulls at Mom's sleeve. When Mom hoists Bailey to her hip with apologies written all over her face, Bailey looks at me again and grins. "Mama. Hi, mama."

I can't form a single word. The only words I have are trailing down my face in streams. All I can do is wave at Bailey and force a smile through my heartache.

Wade peers around the doorway, interrupting at a time that almost feels staged. I need a distraction more than anything else.

"Sorry to break it up in here, but we've got to get this girl to therapy," he says apologetically. "She'll be done at eleven-thirty for lunch. Can I borrow her?"

The way he slows down when he sees the scene in front of him tells me he can sense the tension in the room.

Ready for anything, I move to stand up faster than I probably ever have before. Turning toward my beloved family, I murmur departing words, and without reservation bend to Bailey's head and tenderly kiss her hair. When her hand comes up to rest on my cheek, I don't even feel the throbbing in my spine from bending forward. Frozen in my awkward position, unwilling and unable to move away from her precious touch, I wait until she drops her hand. When she does, after an incredibly slow rise to stand, she lets me take her hand and hold it with both of mine for a short while.

Then she pulls her hand away and there's nothing I can do but turn and walk to the door. Her brief affirmation of me must be held onto with everything I have. It can't be tampered with a bitter goodbye.

Days blend into nights, and bad dreams while asleep blend into nightmares while awake. Confusion and the nearly relentless Hum I forgot about in its absence consume my waking moments when I'm not submerged in therapy. My grasp of days and dates is lost in the constant shuffle of thoughts and what may or may not be recollections of a past that shouldn't have been.

That face haunts me, the one that shouldn't even have existed in my memory. Nothing new comes to me, just the sick knowledge that something either did occur, or almost did, that should not have been.

Oh, one thing came to me.

Time.

I should be elated to have gained the ability to place a timeframe on something from my past. I should shout the newfound reminiscence from the rooftops.

But I can't, not even maybe. It would crush people. Kyle, my steadfast guardian whom God has sent to my side… how can I tell him I might have betrayed him? And then not even be able to tell him for sure if it happened? What would that even sound like?

No, no. I can never tell him, especially not now. He has put his entire existence on hold to be here for me. How could I repay his faithfulness by telling him I may not have returned the favour?

The momentum I have to maintain to get through my therapy load is exhausting. I have nothing left to give anyone or anything. I can't begin to comprehend how I could find more initiative to confess something I don't even understand. It would probably turn my guardian angel away from me with a dagger to his heart.

I float through my therapies in something of a daze. I should always be in a daze, apparently; not overthinking my every move to paralysis seems to catapult me great distances in my recovery. My last physio session took place outside, walking the ups and downs of jagged outdoor paths. Lori and Anne look like they're beside themselves with excitement and pride at my sudden drive and lack of inhibition. Speech therapy doesn't cripple my intellect like it used to; I don't come with enough presence of mind to be bothered by what goes on there. Occupational therapy… well, I can never really fit what I did when I was there into real life, and it flies out of my head as fast as it goes in.

Rattled to the core by my half-memory, I desperately will my circumstances into the nightmare I once so fiercely believed it to be. Not that I believe it so fully to be a nightmare anymore; now I need it to be exactly that. There's no way I could truly have been entertaining the idea of being unfaithful, never mind actually being exactly that, to the one who is giving me everything he has.

This has to be a really bad dream. Nothing more.

"I can't believe you're going back to Manitoba. I can't be two provinces away from my daughter..."

"Come meet me at the tavern."

"Meh, you don't need him. You can figure this out. You're strong and independent."

"...fracture of C1 and C6..."

"...left lobe collapse..."

"...traumatic brain injury..."

"...she might wake up, but she might not ever be the same..."

"...being a functional mother might be a thing of the past for her..."

"Nana, Nana, no Mama."

Disquieting dialogue weaves a tangled web through my thoughts as I feel myself lifting from sleep. I don't have any recollection of what the conversation in my dream was exactly, but I feel entirely unhinged.

As I open my eyes, foreboding coursing through every nerve of my body and soul, I don't allow myself to give attention to anything around me. I don't blink the haze of sleep from my corneas. This ache of disorder is too all-consuming for me to shift any part of my body or awareness.

A bead of fluid strikes my earlobe, lurching me out of my sick trance and into a different level of confusion. Another drop lands on my ear, but much less forcefully. Long minutes or hours of consideration finally tell me that my sweat and tears are trailing off my face and onto my ear.

Tiny scenes materialize behind my unfocused vision. I know these scenes. They have been playing over and over across my heart and mind ever since they first appeared. Not one of those frames ever finishes, though; I can't complete the memories. The only thing I know for sure is that all of these memories are real.

The male face that shows up all the time, the voice I don't quite hear but has an undertone of adultery in its every expression, the sense of betrayal; I even know his name now. That can't be imagined.

I implore the very air I'm breathing to not be real. Raising my hand, I drop it onto my face too hard, trying to jar the reality out of me. I need to not feel it, so that I can know without a doubt that this is the nightmare that plays over and over again like a horror movie jack-in-the-box, and not actually where and what I am.

My hand smashes into my face with all the force of a slap, and whatever dream I need this to be fails miserably. I feel every bit of my hand. Blinking my watery eyes, I reach for my glasses and throw them on to see the time.

3:16. Day or night?

Dark outside. Night.

I mutter a profanity I didn't even know I knew, pushing myself out of bed and shuffling to the bathroom. When I round the corner and hit the light switch, I jump slightly to see a wild-eyed, bony, crazy-haired girl staring back at me. It slowly becomes clear that I've laid eyes on my own reflection. Horrified, I can't tear my eyes away from the mutant in the glass.

My face is gaunt. My eyes are hollow. With my mouth slightly open, the two missing front teeth scream their absence with no apparent shame. My hair looks like a dull knot of tumbleweed. The brace wrapped around my neck and chest reminds me of Frankenstein, although I have no idea if Frankenstein is an actual thing, or if that's just some word that popped into my unstable imaginings.

Unconsciously, my arms move upward with the intention of doing something to restrain my vile hair. But while my left arm moves up to its target, my right shoulder forces that arm to screech to a halt. When it reaches the height of my chest, a startled, pained shriek comes out of my mouth before I can stop it.

It hurts so much. It feels like my arm is being detached from my shoulder at the socket. My left hand jerks toward my right shoulder and tries frantically to push it back together, even though nothing seems to have come apart.

What is this? What else could possibly be wrong with me? Such intense feelings don't ever happen in dreams, no matter how bad they are. The only world I can possibly be in is the real one, no matter how sick this all is.

As I stumble dizzily to sit down on the toilet seat to avoid falling, the night nurse rushes into the room.

"What's going on?" she asks urgently.

"My shoulder," I breathe, alternating between cradling and trying to squeeze it back into place. The more I think about my shoulder, I realize that I haven't ever been able to lie on my right side for more than a few seconds. I've never had the presence of mind to even think about why that might be, but now it's obvious that my shoulder killed that position for me.

When the nurse comes to my side, she gently takes my right arm and pushes it back down. I didn't put it back down after lifting it; it hurt too much to try to move it in any direction. The pain fluctuates between varying degrees of hurt as my arm moves back. My face must be grimacing.

The nurse suddenly has a motherly look to her. "Come, dear, let's get you back to bed. Tell me, what's going on?"

Swallowing my frustration at another ache to add to the endless list, I mutter, "I don't know. I lifted my arm, and it felt like my shoulder broke. I haven't been able to put any pressure on my right side, and I guess it's because my shoulder hurts so much."

The nurse shakes her head sympathetically. "Let me see what I can feel."

I don't immediately allow her to touch my shoulder, but after a short delay I give up on the hope of not adding new problems to the bill.

When she pulls my sleeve down off my shoulder, her expression changes. She sees something, I guess.

Fantastic. What now?

"Well, Amanda, it looks very much like your shoulder is separated."

What does that mean? I look at her questioningly. How could she know anything certain about my shoulder just by looking it at?

"Your collarbone," she continues, "right where it meets your acromioclavicular ligament, is very clearly not where it belongs. It's protruding a fair bit up from your shoulder. I can't believe this has been missed, even during all your sponge baths."

She shakes her head disbelievingly.

I'm stunned. For one thing, I have no idea what she just said. I didn't understand any of it, except that something is way off from where it should be. I truly thought I was getting better, despite how agonizingly slow my progress has been.

"Uh, well... so what now?"

"Dr. Johnson has an MRI scheduled to follow up on your cervical spine. It's very soon, I believe. She'll be here in the morning to discuss it with you, and she'll examine your shoulder."

Her tone has all the affection of a mother speaking to a child. I haven't seen this nurse a whole lot; she apparently only works nights. She's already growing on me—a lot.

"Okay, my dear, you need to get some sleep. Your shoulder will not get any worse overnight, even though we've missed it for so long." She shakes her head hard. "I'm so sorry. I guess there was just so much other vital stuff to look out for, and this was somehow overlooked in the craziness."

I feel really bad for her suddenly. It's not her fault. It's not anyone's fault but my own, really.

"Please, don't be sorry. It's not your fault at all. It's no one's responsibility." The more I say to this nurse, the more I feel like I need to make sure everyone at Riverview knows I'm fully aware that this is all on me. "Only my responsibility," I add firmly.

"Oh no, don't worry about that. Nothing can be done to change what happened." She's talking like a mom again. "We," she points at me and herself, and then makes a general motion toward the entire rehab facility, "are just doing everything in our power to get you healed and self-sufficient again. There's no reason to place any blame. Don't be too hard on yourself."

She glances at her watch.

"It's very late," she says. "Let me get you more sleep aid, and something for the pain. I'll get an icepack too. You were in the bathroom when I came in. Does that mean you finished what you needed to do in there?"

I realize that I still have to pee, and we both move to go. When I get back into bed, the nurse has already returned with a tiny cup of crushed meds and I take it down. With few words, I lay back on the pillow. She arranges an icepack on my shoulder, and then very maternally tucks me in.

A morbidly overactive, too-long pent-up imagination accompanies me until the sleep aid does its job.

Affliction

EXHILARATION CIRCUITS THROUGH ME. IN A FEW MINUTES, I AM leaving Riverview. I'm going in an ambulance to another hospital for an MRI, but that's not the point. I'm leaving Riverview, even if just for a couple of hours. I never thought I'd see the day. The rest of the world outside of this place does exist.

"All right girl, so we're going to have to make sure your neck doesn't get jarred around on the ride over there. You're going to have to lie down on a stretcher in the ambulance." Wade snorts at my disgusted expression. "Hey, I can tell them to turn the sirens on if you're going to give me attitude," he threatens, then bursts into a Wade-like laugh. I can't help but giggle with him.

"Whatever, I can keep pretending to be helpless if it'll get me out of here for a bit." I give Wade a sideways glance, which kicks my double vision into high gear. "Anything for a break from you people."

I can't keep a straight face while I try so hard to fake a jab at him.

Dr. Johnson is standing at the foot of my bed before I even notice she walked in.

"Good morning, Amanda," she greets me with all the professionalism of a doctor, the polar opposite of how Wade and I speak to each other. Her seriousness has grown on me too, somehow, and I grin at her.

"Morning, doc."

Her mouth twitches a little as she looks down at her clipboard. "Okay, Amanda, we're going to take a look at your cervical spine today, and also your acromioclavicular joint. The medical team and I apologize for missing this, but I hope you understand that your more life-threatening injuries took precedence over some of the other parts of your body."

I smile again. "No worries. I didn't even notice it at first." I shrug, feeling the resistance in my shoulder. "Everything hurts; it all just kind of felt the same, I guess."

I can't tell if Dr. Johnson has a reaction to most things I say, and this is another one of those times. I'm not sure if she knows I'm completely crazy and just not telling me, or if she's waiting to see what becomes of my nutcase of a head.

"We're going to need to you go to the ambulance in this." She motions to the stretcher Wade has wheeled into the room. "We need to be sure nothing is aggravated during the transport."

A twinge of anxiety flutters through my core as I'm helped into the stretcher. A guy in some kind of uniform appears just over my head when I'm lying down. He greets me with courteous professionalism before nodding at Dr. Johnson. He takes hold of the stretcher on either side of my head and starts to roll the cot with me on it. Wade calls something out to me as I'm reeled away, but his words don't make it to me.

While we're going down the hall, riding the elevator, and coming to a separate ambulance entrance, the fact that I'm actually about to leave Riverview doesn't feel real, despite going through all the motions. I have been really, really trying to squash the idea that this is all some insanely long dream, but the notion still hangs around in the back of my mind. And where that perception sits, a small part of me is braced for the impact when I find out that I was right the whole time.

Exiting Riverview and approaching the ambulance takes me out of the dreamlike state. The paranoia that escorts me everywhere I go whispers suspicions of where the ambulance will take me. Maybe there's a separate ward of Riverview for crazy people. Maybe they're taking me somewhere they can finally be rid of me.

Another paramedic greets us outside the ambulance and explains again, just like Wade did, the need for the stretcher. This guy throws in a wrench that Wade didn't mention: I have to let them strap my head down ("gently," he keeps on saying) so that it doesn't rock back and forth while the ambulance drives the rutted streets of Winnipeg.

Trying desperately not to betray my mistrust, I force a tight-lipped smile and mutter something that I hope indicates my cooperation. I'm not even sure what I say, I just arrange myself the way he tells me to and find myself lying with my head strapped across the forehead like some rag doll without any will of my own. Dr. Johnson steps into the ambulance, gives another paramedic a clipboard, and says something to him while sizing me up. It seems like she can read me like a book. Her face softens as she bends down and takes my hand.

"Amanda, these paramedics are going to take good care of you," she says, sounding more human than ever before. "We just need to get you to where you're going safely, and then hopefully the MRI will tell us that we don't need to take quite so many precautions. You understand this?"

Never will I leave you; never will I forsake you.

There it is again. An otherworldly calm pours over me, the words replaying in my heart. More miraculous, though, is that rather than being more discomposed than I already am, I feel safe in a rock-solid, protective hold.

My only hope has made Himself known to me, and I finally, truly know it. No matter what happens, He is my only hope, and my God will be here with me if I let Him. My thickly hazed mind can somehow grasp that.

Obviously He can get through the fog in my head. He is God, after all.

For now, I guess the only thing I can do is believe these people. God is telling me that He'll never leave me, and there haven't been any red flags from these people who look like they're trying to help me. No one has lied to me yet, as far as I know.

"Thank you, doc," I breathe. "I think I'm good."

It looks like she has been waiting for some kind of response. I hope she heard me. The ability to put anything more than a whisper behind my words has eluded me, and I know I can't try to voice anything again. Not for a while, at least. How can anyone really speak in the presence of the Almighty? I snap my eyes shut and try to hold onto the fleeting moment.

Dr. Johnson leaving the ambulance goes unnoticed until we're already well on our way. When I finally register that the vehicle is moving, I peel my eyes open and see the paramedic observing me closely.

"Is something wrong?" I ask timidly, not sure if I want an answer.

"No ma'am, don't worry please," he reassures me. "I've just got to make sure there is absolutely no exertion to your neck on this transport."

"Uh… could you use normal words please? I don't get half the stuff you medical people say to me." I hear how ungrateful I sound and quickly add, "I just mean, you are all awesome, but I didn't go to med school. I have no idea what's going on."

"Sorry. Comes with the line of work." The paramedic smiles in good humour. "I'm keeping an eye on your neck. Just making sure it isn't jerked all over the place by these potholed streets, that's all."

I sigh in relief. I've got to just let God handle this. These people are just doing their jobs, which they must be good at.

The ambulance finally slows to a stop and the paramedic moves to get the stretcher freed from whatever fastens it to the floor. The doors open and another uniformed person comes into the light. Soon I am moved outside into the spring air, lying down with my head restrained rather than standing up like a normal person.

I'm not sure what to think of this.

Someone must have mercy on me or something; the strap is loosened and then taken away from my forehead.

"Let's get inside. Don't want her to catch a chill," one of the attendants says as he pushes my cot toward the hospital's entrance.

The sensation of being moved on a stretcher without actually moving must be something I've experienced countless times, but I was obviously unconscious when it happened before. It just feels so weird, especially since I could easily get up and walk on my own. This guy saying they need to get me inside so I don't catch a chill is the weirdest thing ever. I've become nothing more than a twenty-something-year-old toddler.

Well, I'm not wearing a diaper anymore. I'm pretty much potty-trained again, so I guess maybe I'm one up from a toddler.

I snicker a little, and the guy pushing the stretcher looks in my direction. He probably sees delirious people all the time and thinks I'm another one of them.

"Just laughing because I feel exactly like a two-year-old, being pushed around like this," I explain, hoping to rectify his view of me.

He chuckles. "Usually people aren't laughing when they're rolling into the hospital like this, but I see your point."

I hope he's not just saying that. It's not necessarily just this guy's opinion I care about, but everyone who has come into contact with me after I got stuck on this crazy train. I wonder what everyone really thinks of me. Just some insane person, probably.

Never will I leave you; never will I forsake you.

The inrush of these words across my heart is refuge against suspicion. Breathlessly, I mutter a wordless thank you to my Comfort. I feel like I should be shivering in awe, but instead my body and mind are wrapped in brilliant warmth. As I lay prone and basically washed up as far as anyone can see, a feeling of extreme strength and peace embraces me.

"Hi Amanda, I'm Dr. Gilbert." The woman's voice snaps me out of my divine reverie. "How are you? Let's get you prepped for an MRI."

My heart groans out an appeal of sustenance to God while the people surrounding me begin to toy with my CTO. It loosens as they explain that it needs to come off so it won't interfere with the scan. Terrified, I close my mind to the whole process. I can't even comprehend the feeling of no brace around my neck.

Before I realize what's happening, my head is cradled in foam or something, and I'm lying on a narrow table with a huge, rounded white rim just over my head. Dr. Gilbert is explaining the MRI to me. She's saying something about me being inside a scanner for about forty-five minutes, and not to worry, they'll be able to hear me.

Inside of a scanner for forty-five minutes? There is no image in my head other than a photocopier. I can't fathom being inside something like a photocopier, and for almost an hour on top of that.

When Dr. Gilbert motions over my head toward the huge white round thing, she talks about magnets and radio frequency coils. My awareness unconsciously shifts to another level. I start to block her out.

"Amanda. Amanda, do you understand this?"

My thoughts rush back from somewhere I can't pinpoint. Was I supposed to be listening to all this medical jargon?

"I need you to tell me you understand that you've got to hold as still as you possibly can throughout the MRI," Dr. Gilbert stresses, as though repeating herself.

Not knowing what to say, or what I'm really even agreeing to, I grunt a confirmation that I don't know if anyone is able to understand. The doctor seems appeased by it, though, and holds a pair of earplugs toward me.

"Would you prefer earplugs or some music? The machine makes a lot of constant noise that some people find a little bit upsetting …"

She keeps talking but after her comment about normal people being upset by the MRI machine—she must mean people who aren't crazy like me—anxiety rules over me. When she stops talking again, I mutter something about music. I have no idea what's about to happen, but there absolutely cannot be complete silence while my body is photocopied. Someone repeats the command to stay absolutely still, and then I hear a door closing.

Dr. Gilbert must have told me it's go-time, because the thing I'm lying on starts moving into the creepy round white thing. Music suddenly floods the capsule my head is entering. The rest of my body follows my head, and all too soon I'm enclosed by a small, round tunnel that reminds me of something from a horror movie. Again I'm reminded of Frankenstein, but this time the perturbing mental picture is paired with the thought of a faceless monster, prisoner in a science lab.

Dr. Gilbert's voice, sounding distant as though through a telephone receiver, interrupts the music to tell me again to lie extremely still, and then to ask how I'm feeling.

"This is messed up." It's the only thing I can think to say.

"I know it's uncomfortable, but I can hear you all the time. Don't worry, you're not alone."

Now, though, is where this stops being a dream and becomes the actual nightmare I've always known it to be. Ticking, tapping, whirring, and thumping overpower the music. The constant throbbing and feebleness of my neck is the only thing keeping my body still. I'd have been up and out of this inhumane machine the moment my body went into it if I weren't a disabled Frankenstein mutant.

Listing to the machine's blare, mixed with music no person should have to listen to while imprisoned in a narrow cylinder without room to extend my arms to either side, has my heart pounding audibly in my ears. I haven't opened my eyes since I entered the villainous tube, and I won't venture to look around again until I get out. If I get out.

My heart pounds louder and faster, and I'm aware of my breathing too. I sound like I'm panting. I'd be embarrassed if I weren't devastated by how isolated I feel.

So this is what hell is like. Completely forsaken, not a soul around, trapped in a suffocating tiny space, with loud, unfeeling discord surrounding me.

The soft blare of the speaker interrupts my mania.

"Amanda, my dear, you're okay. This is only going to be another few minutes. Four minutes, Amanda. That's all. Just breathe."

The rest of the crazy train passes in an episode of dread in which I'm not even aware of myself. If I speak to anyone again, I have no idea what I'll say, or even if I'll be able to talk.

The drive back to Riverview passes in the same way.

This is the most disgusting dream I've ever had. It's so long. It's never going to end. It had started to feel like maybe, just maybe, this was real life. But after whatever just happened, I can't believe this kind of neurosis could be a real thing. I don't even remember coming back. I'm so wrapped up in myself, and nothing else can find its way into my tiny mind. There's no room.

Seriously, I don't even remember coming back from that stupid MRI. And that was only a few moments ago. Right now, I'm sitting in my room at Riverview, by myself. There's no way I could have gotten here by myself, but I don't remember coming back.

How could I ever have thought otherwise? Of course this ludicrousness is not real. What is real, though? Did I ever even exist?

Revelation

A GENTLE ROUSE PULLS ME OUT OF SOME KIND OF CASTLE IN THE AIR. I feel a smile curve my mouth until I open my eyes and the full awareness of Riverview clouds my aura. My blurry vision meets with a form to my right, throwing my sight into double vision. It still freaks me out every time.

This stupid game my eyes are playing needs to be over. I don't really remember what it feels like to be high, but the thing my eyes are doing must be a throwback to my not-sober days. It's driving me crazier than I already am.

Whoever is beside me comes around to my other side and puts my glasses in my hands.

"Rise and shine, baby girl," an unmistakable voice sings. "We've got a lunch date in the dining hall that you can't miss, or I'll be heartbroken."

Kyle's mom. Janet. This tiny woman has the presence of a whirlwind. Not until this very moment has she been alive in my head, but now that I think of it, I know she has been here a lot. Her image sitting beside my bed, or pacing my room, shrouds my memory. She has loved me while she's been here, too. I think I remember her feeding me several times.

The smile I woke up with slowly returns as I become more awake. A person can't be near Janet without instantly being put in a good mood. Her impulsive, quick, and constant movements, her tongue-in-cheek conversation, and her bottomless energy flood into my memory as I recognize her.

I giggle and she moves closer to me. I pull her closer still.

"Hi," I say, grinning. "Sorry my hair's not done. My makeup isn't on either. I hope you can excuse that."

The moment this leaves my mouth, the person I faced in the mirror the other day flashes back like a slap to the face. As if people are seeing me like that, every day, all the time. My grin vanishes.

"Uh, I really hope you can excuse that." My voice has dropped to almost a whisper. "I look really gross. Sorry."

"Hey, don't be ridiculous. Of course you don't look like the cover of *Vogue*." My memory of her always-smiling face holds true. I wouldn't know any other face of hers. "You look like you got hit by a truck and then got up and walked away from it. You look like a superstar. Don't be ridiculous."

Her eyes sparkle before she turns away and grabs a hoodie of mine that's hanging over a chair. She hands it to me and waits for me to put it on.

"Let's go get you some grub, baby girl." She holds her hand out and I take it, following her toward the dining hall.

As we pass the nurse's desk, Wade jumps up.

"Hey, girl, how are you doing?" He looks at me expectantly, and I guess that means I'm supposed to know that he's referring to something specific. At my smile and tiny nod, he just shakes his head. "Your MRI this morning? I got wind that you were a little overwhelmed. It's all good now, though?"

Memories of my panic rush back. I stop in my tracks and shudder at the thought of that confining tunnel. Wade clears his throat to prompt an answer.

"Wade, I'm telling you, don't ever make me do that again," I state with all the fierceness my throat can squeeze out. For a split second, his and Janet's faces are veiled with shocked amusement. My own face cracks into a smirk. "I mean, that's just plain cruel. That's the kind of stuff that makes me think this is a bad dream or that I'm actually insane."

"Baby girl," Janet croons as though singing a lullaby, "people have MRIs all the time. People who aren't insane. They're pretty normal. You are very special, but you're not special enough that you're the only person to ever have one of those."

Her singsong voice decreases my paranoia of the day's events.

"Well, this sucks," I groan. "I was wondering if I lost my mind. I guess I did." I turn to face Kyle's mom. "I'm so sorry that your son's fiancé and your grandbaby's mom is now actually psychotic."

Even to myself, I sound like I'm just joking around. The sick thing is, I'm not joking at all. The knowledge of my insanity does make it a little easier to swallow the events of my course in Riverview, though. I'd rather be crazy than forever trapped in purgatory.

"Hey," Wade interrupts. "Girl, quit being so hard on yourself. You're not crazy or dreaming or any of that garbage, Amanda. MRIs are hard for a lot of people who feel claustrophobic in the machine. But you, you're not insane. You had brain trauma that's made you have to learn most of life again, and twenty-one years of functioning has mostly come back in not even two months. So get off your high horse," he chuckles at himself, "and just chill out already. You're not going to get hit by a truck and just get up and walk away right from where you left off. Give yourself a little grace already. And accept where you are."

His last few words stay on repeat while I eat lunch. As I take a tiny sip of my normal, non-thickened water, without choking and spluttering it all over myself, I remember the process of drinking normal water again. Glancing at the plate in front of me, filled with real food that hasn't been pureed to baby food consistency, I think about the gruelling process of learning to chew and swallow real food, and walking, and using the bathroom, and pushing full sentences out of my spinning head. I remember the people I have spent my whole life with—

Janet sits across from me, reading a newspaper, sipping at coffee. She can't possibly know how much I'm affected by her doing something as normal as reading the paper and drinking coffee. My eye catches a headline on the front page of the open paper: *2 Murdered, 3 in Hospital Following Break and Enter.* I blink hard and read it again.

In nightmares, bad things happen never happen to other people, especially not other people I don't know and whose devastated lives won't impact me. If life can change so dramatically and destructively for other people in the world, yet it still goes on, I guess my own life will go on too. Even if it doesn't, life for my family will go on. Their entire lives aren't devoted to me. There's so much more to it than the bricks and mortar surrounding me.

I can't believe it's taken me this long to finally accept that this is where I am. The only way to move on is to pull up my socks and get on with it. Whatever they're doing here, they're doing for my benefit. They don't have to—they could just worry about their own survival like I've been obsessing about mine—but they're still doing everything they can to help me get back onto my feet.

The drive to keep going with all the momentum my body and soul can create permeates me. I feel the urge to laugh, to rub off the goofy look I know is probably plastered all over my face.

"Thanks for reading the paper," I say suddenly. I giggle at the absurdity of my own words. "I mean, it's really good to see real life in here, even if it's just words on a page. I just realized how much I need to stop being so self-absorbed. How are you doing?"

Janet beams. "I'm wonderful, thanks! Especially hearing you right now, this is amazing! I bet you'll go home in a couple of weeks!" At my doubtful expression, she adds, "Just you wait, you'll see."

When I'm alone in my room later, the old familiar feelings of desolation and hopelessness don't overtake me like before. Instead, I'm motivated to truly live again. I wander into the bathroom in search of the toiletries bag I've seen lying on the counter. Rooting through it for a toothbrush, I come across some makeup.

With my toothbrush, moisturizer, and makeup spread on the vanity, I flex my jaw in preparation for the tightness I know I'll face when I try to brush my own teeth. The impact of the accident made my jaw unable to open too widely, and I guess the CTO cradling my throat and pushing on my jawline doesn't help. For as long as I can remember, nurses have been using a little piece of foam to temperately clean my teeth behind my slightly parted lips. In the past couple of days, I've finally started doing it myself. I'm disgusted at how my teeth haven't been fully, correctly brushed since I've been here.

They tell me my revulsion with myself shows huge progress in the recovery of my mental capacity. I'm not really sure how, though.

It's ridiculous that I'm nervous about brushing my teeth. I smile wildly at my reflection, baring my teeth. The unnaturally huge smile hurts, not only in the feeling but in the look of my whole face. The unkempt, wild-looking girl in the mirror looks like she's never lifted a finger to her own face or hair, driving me into action. I put too much toothpaste on the toothbrush to make up for lost time.

My jaw screams its protest, opening further than it's been forced to yet. The constant gagging and exaggerated soreness is somehow welcome. I'd rather be doing normal things in discomfort than lying in bed, staring at the clock for days without end.

When I come around to the makeup part of my forgotten morning ritual, I feel excitement at the bottle of foundation in my hand. It's the weirdest, yet most logical sensation. The skin on my face is riddled with red marks and little glass scars. Dr. Johnson's face floats into my recollection with an explanation of my hormones going into overdrive as a result of brain trauma, resulting in an extreme case of acne.

I don't need to remember how I used to apply makeup; it's easy enough to know that I just smear it all over my face and add concealer to the countless imperfections that dot my skin. When I finish, I comb through the bag of toiletries in search of a ponytail holder. I find one and try to run a hand through my ghastly mane; the slick, grimy, knotted feeling of unwashed and uncombed hair makes me gag again. It's so revolting that I have to get it restrained.

I lift my arms to tie it back. When my right arm reaches the height of my shoulder, it moves no farther. It feels like razor-sharp claws tear into it. I yelp and clamp my left hand over my mouth as I slowly lower the useless arm. I hope no one heard me, even though I'm sure someone did.

It only takes a few seconds before Wade rounds the corner.

"Girl, you can't be making noises like that if you don't want people checking up on you in the bathroom," he mutters sarcastically. When he looks at my face, though, his expression softens and he backs away from the bathroom door.

I follow him out into the room and sit at the edge of my bed.

"Getting ready for a date with your man, are you?" he comments, leaning against the wall. "You're looking good."

"Ugh. Quiet, Wade. I know you've seen this rat's nest on my head. Why aren't you people washing my hair?" I make myself laugh so he knows I'm half-joking. "I should complain to the board of directors or something. I'm an embarrassment to Riverview."

"Hey, listen here. One, you're beautiful, we're proud of you, and you're not even *maybe* an embarrassment to Riverview. You've come miles from where you were when you got here. Two, we can't wash your hair for a couple of reasons: your neck is broken, and you're wearing a CTO that can't come off. The CTO can't get wet, and there'd be no way to keep it dry if we washed your hair."

It doesn't matter how serious Wade is, he can't manage a gruff or unkind tone of voice. I've always heard a smile in his voice, no matter what he says. It makes me want to be happy every time. It's not just a coincidence that he's here. God put him here. He knew what I needed in this madhouse.

"All right, fine. You win." I raise a hand in mock submission. "If you people don't want to be responsible for breaking my neck again, I guess I get it."

Wade grins. "I always knew you were a reasonable person. But it might help you to know that we'll get your MRI results back the day after tomorrow, and hopefully it'll show that your spine is healed enough to remove the CTO. It'll be for short amounts of time at first, because it'll be hard for you to support your head after the CTO did it for so long. And then," he pauses and raises his eyebrows at my sick hair, "maybe someone can wash your hair."

Whoa. I can't imagine not wearing the CTO, which has been the bane of my existence for so long. It's a necessary evil, and I hardly notice it anymore. I think Lori or Anne has told me that it'll come off soon, and I'm pretty sure my reaction was pretty much what it is now.

Terror. Incompetence. Helplessness.

Never will I leave you; never will I forsake you.

As fast as the panic comes, it's replaced with the words of my Comforter. The swift rush of peace brings heat to my eyes, but I blink fast before anything spills over.

I need to talk to God. He's been all over this place—and everywhere I've been since I drove into that semi, He's been there too. I have been so close to falling off so many ledges, but He always pulls me back into his arms.

The whole time, though, I haven't been talking to Him. Yeah, maybe I was too unconscious, and then too dazed, to even think about praying. But from the moment I became able, I should have been praising, thanking, and seeking Him.

I can do that now. Even though my brain has been literally rattled until everything it held was shaken out of it, some of the most important things have come back. The knowledge of my Only Hope has been the most significant one.

My face feels hot all over again, and I know there's no point in trying to hold anything back. I look up at Wade, who's observing my face with open curiosity. I smile sheepishly.

"Sorry, Wade," I offer shakily, my voice failing to hide my urge to cry. "Do you mind if I just chill out by myself for a bit?"

"For sure." He nods, stepping in the door's direction. "Take all the time you need, girl."

Alone with my Maker, I drop onto my bed and let my heart cry out to Him.

Messenger

THE DRONE OF THE TV IN FRONT OF ME AND THE SOFA BRING FEELINGS of familiarity I can't really place. Something feels so right, so constant. I stare at the TV but don't see or hear what's on it. I don't care to, either. This alien moment of comfort can't be torn away from me, and I cringe away from the shadow that crosses the doorway of the dining hall.

"Amanda."

I pretend I don't hear him. The sound of my name hurts, even if it means someone is here to see me. My instant of peace, of feeling at home, has been shattered.

Home.

I freeze as the word crosses my thoughts.

This reminds me of home. I can't picture or fathom home, but somehow that's exactly what this moment characterizes.

"Amanda."

The same male voice behind me, a voice I know but don't know.

Pained at the tearing away of my sense of home in this barren wasteland, I draw out a blink, savouring the feeling before it flees.

"Hi," I say softly, still unsure who my guest might be. He sits down at the other end of the sofa. I have to shift my entire torso to move my head, which takes me a lot longer than it should.

The possibility of learning to live without the CTO flits across my considerations, making it even more difficult to figure out who this man is. I'm so bad at living. I can't seem to think.

"Hi, Amanda," he says, tearing me out of some distant reflection. I fix my contemplation on him.

When his face comes into focus, I feel a wave of refreshment.

"Hi, um…" I stop sheepishly, unable to give him a name. "Sorry, I'm so sorry…"

"Don't be sorry, Amanda. I'm Pastor Glen."

Oh! Pastor Glen! I don't know exactly what you mean to me, but I know it's a lot.

Looking at him with unrecognized fellowship, it occurs to me that maybe I haven't said anything. Maybe I just thought it.

Probably, because he isn't responding to anything I think I said.

"Hi Pastor," I offer self-consciously. "Sorry."

"There is absolutely nothing to apologize for."

Good-naturedness pours out of his every word, and the feeling of home surrounds me once again. Images flutter across my internal vision with a bittersweet swell: Pastor Glen standing at the pulpit, and then sitting with his wife and me in deep conversation.

"Wow," I breathe, awed by the new memories. "I remember you. I mean, I remember certain times with you and… Karen? Your wife? You were my friends."

His wife's face infiltrates the often blurry slate of my consciousness. These two, these extraordinary mentors in my life… I don't need to recall every memory of them to know they have been Godsends.

"We are your friends, Amanda. Never forget that," Pastor Glen says earnestly. "It is so humbling that you can remember us as your friends."

I'm mortified at having an important guy like Pastor Glen make the effort to give me some company, especially once it finally, truly occurs to me that he is the head pastor of the church I went to once upon a normal life. This abnormally normal occurrence is the strangest mixture of thrill and shame.

"Pastor Glen," I state abruptly, trying to put some strength in my voice. "Thank you for coming. I really, really appreciate it. But… don't you have more important stuff to do? I'm just lying up here in a hospital bed; aren't there so many more people who need you?"

My fake confidence dwindles pretty quickly, and by the last few words I'm almost whispering.

Before he can respond, I gain a second wind. "If I'm not dying any-more, shouldn't I be helping people like you are? So many people have helped me so much already. I should be good to go and not stealing anyone else's attention. I should just suck it up and be like a normal person who doesn't need everyone to bend over backwards for me."

The fact that I'm panting when I finish doesn't help my case, and I feel my face flush.

Pastor Glen looks at me with all the compassion of a father. He passes his Bible back and forth between his hands.

"Right now this is about God and you." His face is alight with exhilaration. "He kept you alive because He so clearly has huge plans for you. I'm here because I want to be here for a fellow child of God who needs companionship more than she needs most things. We are God's children, and you are my sister. My sister needs someone to be here. There's nowhere I'd rather be, Amanda."

Looking at him is too hard; he's too good to be here for me. I drop my eyes to the floor and mutter my thanks, hoping he doesn't leave and at the same time hoping he does.

The only words I can think to say come flying out of my mouth. "I need all the help I can get right now."

"Amanda, the Holy Spirit is helping you more than you could possibly know." His words are doused with new vibrancy as he collects his thoughts. "Can I tell you a story about you in the hospital?"

At a loss for anything to say, I just wait.

"When you were in the ICU, you had been out of a coma for a number of days but were pretty unresponsive to most things. You'd squeeze your parents hands' when they talked to you, but your eyes wouldn't focus on anything and you hadn't said a word since you regained consciousness. I came to sit with you and read God's Word, believing that He could open your heart to anything He wanted you to hear, even if it felt to you like I was reading Greek."

He almost laughs at this point. Even though I know there's more to his story, I can't guess where he's going. I need him to finish so I know he's not laughing at me.

"Did something happen?" I ask impatiently.

Pastor Glen smiles broadly at my childishness. "I was switching back and forth between reading different stories of God's healing and Psalm

103:1–5, over and over again. I repeated this for probably an hour. Remember, you hadn't said a word to anyone yet at this point."

Appearing slightly overcome, he stops for a minute.

"Amanda, do you know what happened? Let me tell you how great our God is. The Holy Spirit knows the utterings of your heart, and He gave you words. After almost an hour of me reading from the Gospels and Psalm 103, you spoke. For the first time since you woke up from your coma, you spoke."

The serenity of his face could tell no lie. God spoke to him too in that moment, this much I can see. But how?

"Amanda, your first words were, 'Jesus, Jesus, love Jesus, love Jesus.'"

I feel my mouth hanging agape as I process what he just told me. I don't remember anything before I woke up here at Riverview. Not even the move from the hospital. I don't remember meeting anyone, and I hardly recall not being able to walk or use the bathroom.

What I do remember, what encompasses me still, is feeling completely and utterly lost, hopeless, and unbelieving. I remember feeling like reality had vanished from my grasp, and knowing that I wouldn't be able to find it again, no matter what I did. I don't even know what reality is, what to look for. For all I know, I may never have known reality. Maybe I was always here, nothing but a shadow of someone else's life.

Yet here is Pastor Glen, who I know and trust more than anything in this moment, telling me that my first words after I flirted with death were worship to the only One who truly has me. When I knew nothing and no one, I knew God. When I didn't know that I knew God, the Holy Spirit knew my heart and spoke for me.

Only when a box of tissue is held out to me do I feel the wetness on my face and the heaving of my shoulders. Lost in awe at how the Master of the Universe works, I don't really hear what Pastor Glen says next. Then my silent, overwhelmed worship is accompanied by the lyrics he's reading from the open Bible in his hands:

> Praise the Lord, my soul;
> all my inmost being, praise his holy name.

Praise the Lord, my soul,
and forget not all his benefits—
who forgives all your sins
and heals all your diseases,
who redeems your life from the pit
and crowns you with love and compassion,
who satisfies your desires with good things
so that your youth is renewed like the eagle's.

—Psalm 103:1–5

Sitting at the table in my room after nightfall with the Bible open in front of me, I gape at the thousands of characters on the page. I've been reading the same passage over and over for the longest time, but I can't remember what I just finished reading the second I move on to the next verse.

Pastor Glen left me some verses and passages to look up that could offer me hope, but it took me forever just to find the first one on the list. Apparently I forgot how the Bible works. Not only that, but the ability to retain the words I've read completely eludes me. I feel irritated at my incompetence, to the point that it takes everything in me not to slam the holy book closed.

"Lord, Father…" No other words come to me. I'm aching inside and out; the emptiness of my heart has an almost tangible throb that surges up to the only One who can hear it. The impulse to put my head down into my arms infuriates me even more. There's no way I can get myself into this most natural position because of the CTO.

The urge to scream builds so fast, the few depressing things I know circling my mood like a whirlwind. Sweat runs down my forehead even while I shiver with the coldness encompassing me.

I have to go somewhere else before I lose my mind.

I stand up fast, forcing myself to pause and hold onto the table before my head rush blows me over. After the strangest, slowest pause, I finally feel grounded enough to keep moving. I grab the housecoat slung over the back of the chair I just rose from, shrug it on, and pace the room a few times.

Even with no destination in mind, I find myself veering toward the hallway and not stopping when I leave the room. Seeing the nurse's desk halts me for a split second; I then see the night nurse on the phone with her back to me. As silently as I can, I move past her and keep walking into the seemingly endless hall. When the elevators are close, I feel no urge to leave Riverview and try to get away. I keep walking past them.

When I reach the end of the hall, I just turn around and keep walking. The nurse's desk comes into view, and I turn and walk the other way again. I pace the hall for an unknown length of time, my thoughts finding an outlet they've never had before.

Be still and know that I am God.

Stopping in place, I can't make myself lift even a toe to keep moving. I will never get used to this calming shock. It falls on me every time I hear words like this spoken into my soul.

Be still and know that I am God. I will be exalted among the nations. I will be exalted in the earth.

My racing mind loses its momentum and swirls to a stop. In place of all the racing, only one thought lingers, like a gentle sigh on its way out. So mildly that I could easily let it slip away, I realize that this is only a blip on God's timeline of His holy purpose for me. Holding onto the thought expands it, and it's soon followed by the knowledge that no matter what happens to me or anyone else, it can all be used to glorify the God of heaven and earth.

"Amanda!" a voice ahead calls with urgency.

Startled out of my peaceful musing, I look up to see the night nurse coming toward me. With a sharp intake of oxygen, I take a step toward her.

"Where are you going?" she asks. "What are you up to? Is everything okay?"

At the sound of her tone, more concerned than angry, I come back from my dumbstruck state.

"Hey, sorry if I freaked you out," I mumble. "I couldn't relax in my room. I guess I just felt like I needed to walk off my weird feeling or something." It occurs to me that she might think I was trying to leave. They tell me I tried that once before. "Oh please don't think I was trying to walk away from here. I just needed to move around without someone over…"

I trail off, not wanting to sound thankless.

"Seriously, I was just walking the hallway," I start again. I have no idea what the look on her face means. "I passed the desk and you were on the phone. That was probably a while ago. I don't know how long, but I just walked up and down the hall the whole time. I needed to be in a place that wasn't my room. It's so lonely in there."

Her face breaks into a soft smile, lifting a weight of worry off of me. "I guess it's okay, my dear." She rubs her face. "I saw the light still on in your room so I went to check in on you. When I saw your empty bed, my heart pretty much stopped." She laughs nervously. "I can't lose you on my watch. I was so terrified. But as soon as I walked out of your room to call someone, I saw you way down the hall. At least I was pretty desperate for it to be you. I'm so glad it is."

She lets out a relieved huff of air as she extends her hand to me in hopes that I'll go with her. I grin at her, thankful. She steps in my room's direction and looks over her shoulder at me; I take that as my cue to follow.

After the nurse leaves me to myself in my bed, I close my eyes and ponder the incredible revelation I experienced in the hall. The fact that it comes back to me so quickly, without me practically breaking a sweat from thinking so hard, is enough for me to know that God is undeniably speaking to me in this entire jumble. Even if God's words aren't audible, they've been written all over my heart so clearly.

He is not finished with me. There is more than this.

Initiation

"AMANDA, MY GIRL, DR. JOHNSON'S GOT SOME NEWS FOR YOU!" LORI hoots as she barrels into my room behind the lady pushing the breakfast cart. She utters a quick apology to the breakfast lady for coming up behind her so fast, then moves past her without slowing down. She stops short at the foot of my bed, her grin stretching ear to ear. "I can't wait for her! Amanda, your CTO—that vice can come off!"

Whoa.

Lori teeters, giddy with excitement while anticipating my response. I have no response, though. Only a dizzying wave of mixed emotions that crashes on me and cements my mouth shut.

I hate this thing. This spinal prison has been the most infuriating, uncomfortable, and frustrating invasion on my body and my freedom to move like a human. While I have loathed every moment that this brace has assaulted me with its claws, I have also depended on it like the nastiest vice. I can't imagine not having it. I need it. Even though I have dreamt of the day I can burn it, I need it.

"Amanda," Lori says softly. I look up at her thoughtful face with nothing of my own to say. "How do you feel about that? What's going on in that beautiful head of yours?"

A rush of words comes to me. Before I can filter it, I squeak, "I can't not have it. I won't know what to do. I have no idea how to keep my neck straight. It'll break all over again the second this thing comes off." My voice starts to quiver. I'm so embarrassed, but I'm also terrified, so I just keep talking. "Is someone going to hold on to the top of my head when it gets taken off so that my face doesn't fall into my chest? I swear, anything that has healed is going to go right back to where it was. If I just think about not wearing it, I can pretty much feel how impossible it'll be to not have something holding my neck in line. I don't know how to do it."

I run out of words when I run out of air, but knowing how crazy I already sound, I suppress a gasp. My incompetence is nothing new, but it doesn't hurt any less when it rears its disgusting head. If it were possible to hang my head in shame, I would. I can only close my eyes instead.

Lori's hand falls gently on mine as she perches on the side of my bed. I look up at her and don't see her feeling sorry for the chump in front of her like I awkwardly expect she might. Instead she looks like she's suppressing childish excitement on the morning of a birthday.

"Amanda, I know you're nervous, but woman, you decided to walk again after you got crushed by a truck that probably weighed eighty thousand pounds." Her eyes shine with confidence. "You have proven to everyone how resilient you are, and now you just need to open your eyes and believe it yourself. You've got this."

"Yes, my dear. Do you hear Lori?" Dr. Johnson's voice sounds from the doorway. How long has she been there?

"Dr. Johnson, hi! I had to tell Amanda. I couldn't wait for you," Lori says, sounding sheepish. She and the doctor both laugh at her mock apology.

"Amanda, we've got to remove the brace," Dr. Johnson says firmly, but not irritably. "We can't have you developing a psychological dependence on it, which you already have begun to do. We need to stop that in its tracks. The MRI showed us that your spinal fractures have fused, so that means it is time to remove the CTO."

They both sound… happy. Enthusiastic, maybe. Well, I guess if Dr. Johnson is in on this, it must be okay. She wouldn't tell Lori to tell me the brace could come off if it actually couldn't. I'm not really sure what she's telling me, but at least I get that she says it's okay for the CTO to be gone. My spine is fused. That means back together, right?

Good grief. Just trust them. They know this, I don't. And anyway, I've been desperate for this moment since I woke up in this corruption of life. They keep telling me that I took the brace off myself once. If I could do that when I was less mentally stable than I am right now, of course I'll be fine.

"Ugh, okay, fine, take it off of me," I say. "I've hated this thing. I still do. Just take it."

I sit up straighter, if that's possible with the awful board along my spine, and clench my fists. Thinking about it, my fists won't have anything to do with keeping my head from falling off. Releasing my fists, I flex my fingers instead, trying to imagine what it must be like to just be a person who wears a shirt on her back. I can't even wear a normal shirt. When I wanted to stop wearing the ugly hospital gowns all day, every day, Mom brought me giant t-shirts. She cut slits up the backs of them to accommodate the wretched CTO. I haven't been able to wear decent clothes, wash my hair, or sleep on my stomach for months because of this beastly thing.

"That's the spirit," Dr. Johnson says approvingly. "I believe Wade has informed your family about this landmark in your recovery. This will be a big day."

"You got it, doc," Wade bellows as he strides into the room with my mom and dad behind him.

Everyone looks so elevated and excited that I can't help but feel a little more confident. They're all so certain and cheerful about the thought of me getting rid of this thing. They've all been so harsh about my supposed removal of the CTO on my own, and I guess I started to mirror their military strictness. Now they're unrelenting about it coming off. Everything is so confusing all the time.

"Okay, let's do this thing. Ready, Amanda?" Lori gently pulls on my arm so that I reposition myself with my back to her. "Let your instincts take over. You know how to do this; you've been holding your head up for two decades before this."

"It is vital that you keep your back straight," Dr. Johnson jumps in. "This CTO forces you into good posture, but when it comes off, it'll feel natural to slump your spine. Don't do that. Makes sure you practice good posture. If you don't, your back and neck will ache constantly. You'll be prone to stiffness in your neck and upper back now because of the trauma you've faced, but you can offset that a lot by maintaining good posture."

"Uh, got it, I think." I giggle nervously at their orders. I should just know how to handle myself. I'm in my twenties; I shouldn't be learning to hold my head up.

"Ready then, girl?" Dad says with a bounce in his voice, his eyes shining with pride. I saw my parents come in, but it didn't really register that they were here until my dad spoke. My mind is too busy with other stuff, like relearning humanity.

"Hi Dad," I squeak.

He just smiles as he and Mom come closer. Dad watches protectively as Lori and Wade fiddle with the CTO entwined around my back, chest, neck, and chin. Mom looks into my eyes. Her teary, beaming face has all the love in the world on it.

Lori and Wade twitch the CTO for a minute. Lori then repeats the instructions about posture and instinct. She then counts back from five.

"…three, two, one." The tiniest, longest pause follows before the choke-hold I've come to know so well is released. It happens so fast that it feels like my entire upper body is going to liquefy. I can only think to keep my head where it is, and do whatever it takes to not let myself drop even fractionally.

The ironic, relieved pain swirling through my top half reminds me not to let my neck flop over. How could I forget to maintain a fully erect pose when my backbone never shuts up? It's howling its frailty with its every vertebra. Hoots and cheers accompany me as I very slowly stand up; Lori prods me to walk with her down the hall to try out this new chapter of independence. I feel like a pillowcase with the pillow taken out. At the same time, though, the air on my neck feels like a soft breeze against clammy skin that hasn't seen the light of day for months.

As I walk past others who only know me inside of the hideous CTO, they do a double take. I can only imagine how different I look. Feeling all eyes on me and hearing congratulations from people I don't know, it starts to dawn on me what's truly happening: I have graduated out of the neck brace. I am one massive step closer to leaving this firestorm behind. Despite not being able to turn my head more than an inch beyond what the brace allowed, I gingerly rotate my neck as far as it'll go, grinning stupidly.

Never will I leave you; never will I forsake you.

Tears slip past my eyelids when the promise of my only Hope whispers into my soul. He has never left me. He has never forsaken me. Even when I haven't been capable of seeking Him, He let me find Him.

My God is real love.

Probation

FINALLY, AFTER ALL THIS TIME, THE RHYTHM OF RIVERVIEW HAS become known to me. I wake up one day with the ability to recall the previous day's events, and the capacity doesn't go away. Every therapy session catapults me forward to a new level of functionality. It's like school: morning to afternoon classes, with a lunch break in there somewhere, except instead of learning academics the curriculum is the basics of life. One of those basics is working to bring the motion of my neck back to a functional range.

It's been nine days since they took the CTO off (the ability to give this a timeframe is the most stupidly exciting thing in the world). At first I had no choice but to put the contraption back on every now and then because the ten-pound weight of my head is a shock to my neck muscles. But I told the nurses when I needed it. The first time, I begged for it because I just couldn't keep on holding my morbidly heavy head on my shoulders. The first few times it was allowed to happen very easily, but every time after that the story changed and I had to convince them to let me. This feels like a head trip all over again. I basically wasn't supposed to even touch the brace while I wore it, and I hated every minute of it, but the second it came off, it's not supposed to be on me at all if I can help it. I feel like an extension of my body is missing.

"Hey beautiful." Mom peers into the open bathroom door.

I stand in front of the mirror and examine my ashen, patchy face, cringing at the tornado of hair on my head.

"Hi Mom." I can't return her exuberance at the same time as I behold the girl in the mirror. My forced smile seems to add to her eagerness, though.

"I've got some news for you, my girl," she says through a megawatt smile.

When I focus on Mom, she's practically vibrating. What could be so exciting in this mental hospital?

"I don't know what to tell you first! Do you want the good news or the even better news?"

So taken aback by the possibility of good things, I just step back. I don't know if I've gotten good news here before; I don't remember what it feels like to hear something good. Even the news about the CTO's end was hampered by my self-doubt.

"Okay, well I'll just go in order then." She steps toward me and takes both of my hands. "One, we're going to wash your hair today, and two, you're coming home for the weekend!"

After a long, silent, stunned shock, all I can think to say is, "What day is it?"

"Friday. Amanda, today! You're coming home today after your therapies are done this afternoon! We'll pick Bailey up from daycare when we get back to town!" Mom is whispering and yelling at the same time, struggling to contain herself. "You're done eating lunch, right? You have forty-five minutes before speech therapy, so there's time right now to wash your hair. I brought a bathing suit for you to change into right now; me and a nurse are going to help you out with your hair, okay?" She puts the suit down on the counter and, looking like a kid on Christmas morning, gives me a peck on the cheek before leaving the bathroom and pulling the door closed behind her.

As I get changed, not sure about how I feel about being bathed by two other people, what Mom just said starts to sink in. My hands shake so hard. Clumsier than usual, it takes me twice as long to change.

When I finally emerge from the bathroom, a sweet female nurse I recognize waits beside Mom. She greets me and explains briefly how she's going to strap me into some kind of mechanical thing that will lower me into the tub, then leads Mom and me down the hallway to a different, massive bathroom.

Everything becomes a little blurry once I'm about to hit the bath. It's pretty obvious that I'll need all the help I can get. That doesn't make it any less awkward, though, and I just close my eyes and let it happen once I'm strapped into the contraption that will hold me in place in the water. The nurse mentions that although my spine is fused now, it's still touchy. I need to make sure there's not a lot of agitation where my spine is concerned; therefore, the imprisoning bath device.

Blocking it out as I am, I don't really feel the luxury of the warm bathwater or the scalp massage as my rancid hair is finally scrubbed clean. When I'm out and back in my room with a clean head of hair, though, the fresh scent wafting to my nose makes me wonder exactly how my hair smelled before this.

"Um, Mom, I probably don't want to know, but how long has it actually been since my hair was washed? How long have I been here, anyway?"

The question has been lingering at the back of my mind, but I've stuffed it down, just trying to remain in ignorant bliss, not wanting to hear someone actually say the words. Well, it would be a lot more blissful to know that there might be an end in sight.

Mom's eyes are a minefield of emotions as she gingerly combs her fingers through my tangled, wet hair.

"Today is June 19. The accident happened on April 22. You've been here for almost two months. Your hair hasn't been washed." She breaks up her solemn face with a tension-releasing giggle. "I know you understand why."

Going through the afternoon's therapies with the aroma of shampoo floating around my head is easier and faster than it's ever been. I know there's something else incredible on the horizon, but I can't remember what that other thing is. I'm perfectly content, though, knowing my head doesn't stink like it must have before. While I'm glad I never really noticed a smell, I can't help but wonder what other people made of it.

At 4:30, I stroll back into the ward that has been my home for two months, and Mom's words slowly crawl back to the forefront of my mind. I don't remember what day it is, but she said I'd get to go home for the weekend. I get to be with my little girl for the whole weekend.

I am going home. Chills run up and down my entire body with the incredible possibility that Riverview will not be all I ever see.

What if I wake up now, though? What if I actually was dreaming the whole time? What if—

"Amanda!" Mom shrieks when I enter my room. "Amanda, home time!"

She gestures at a backpack that looks packed and ready to go. I exhale hard, releasing the breath I've been holding in nervous anticipation since I stepped off the elevator and onto my floor.

This is really happening. I am really going home.

Flurries of people come in and out of the room, giving orders and suggestions to Mom and me. Dr. Johnson comes in last as Tom is putting the CTO back on me for the car ride. They tell me there is absolutely no question; I will need to wear the brace in vehicles to keep my spine in line for at least six more weeks. She gives Mom and me a stern set of instructions about not overdoing anything, not taking stairs, not stepping into a shower, not this, not that. Then she reaches the end of her don'ts, and her face relaxes.

"Have a wonderful time," she says, her voice suddenly going soft.

Mom and I look at each other with thrilled suspense, waiting for dismissal.

"Can I take her home now?" Mom asks, her polite tone not betraying her impatience.

Dr. Johnson laughs happily and nods. It's awesome. I feel like I haven't seen her laugh, which might make sense; I probably haven't been a cup of tea while I've been here.

As Mom and I make our way outside, Tom escorting us, I pinch myself over and over again. This needs to be real. I walk faster and have to restrain myself from rushing Mom. We need to get in the car and start driving before someone comes running out of the building to say I have to stay here after all.

When we're finally in the car, belted and ready to go, Tom pokes his head in my open window and repeats the instructions Dr. Johnson gave me. I don't hear a word he says. The exhilaration of not only being outside the walls of Riverview, but in a getaway vehicle, has muted all the pain that constantly riddles my spine, amplifying the music of the world.

Tom steps back from the car and waves, and Mom pulls out of her parking spot faster than she probably should. I giggle at her unconcealed delight. I love my mom.

In a fantastic turn of events, I'm in a car driving away from Riverview. Unreal. I can't believe it. I'm spellbound by the scenery that's nothing more than the city of Winnipeg and nothing less than what I've been yearning for with every fibre of my being. I appreciate more than anything that Mom is silently letting me take it in. I can't look at any one thing; there's so much more to this beautiful world than I remember. Trees, houses, stores, offices, traffic lights, people, more people, leashed dogs, sunlight… the life I've been missing is painfully beautiful.

The backdrop of God's green earth along the highway outside the city trumps everything I saw before it. Mom continues to let me gape at the world; I can see the joy all over her face out of the corner of my eye.

"Mom…"

She steals a sideways glance at me and grabs my hand. "What's up, darling?"

"Mom, I… wow…"

What do I even say? There's no one word or sentence, or even entire speech, that could fully communicate what I'm feeling right now.

"Yes, my dear, I know," she agrees fervently. She's always reading my mind. Mom knows me so well. The rest of the drive home passes in the same companionable silence it started out with, yet I feel like we've been having the best conversation.

Driving into my hometown, and then into the parking lot of Bailey's daycare, I feel the most bittersweet sentiment. When Mom asks if I want to stay in the car while she gets Bailey, I quickly agree. I'm not up for going inside and fielding so many questions. I just want to get my baby and go home.

Mom returns in record time with a sweet little girl in her arms. With mixed emotions of joy and heartache, I turn around as far I can while she buckles Bailey into her car seat.

"Hi monkey," I say softly to my precious girl.

Bailey just stares at me for a long minute, and I can't tear my eyes away from hers in spite of the sensation of burning coals along my backbone.

Mom climbs back into the car and backs out of the parking lot. I stay where I am, ignoring the pain and grinning at my girl like an idiot.

"Nana, Mama?" Bailey finally asks, unsure.

After a short pause, she squeaks, "Mama. Hi Mama!"

Ecstasy rings through my ears right to my heart. Whether it's just the name she knows or she remembers me as her mommy is irrelevant at this point. My daughter is calling me Mama. I can't even remember the last time I heard that word in her sweet voice.

When the house I lived in before I came to Riverview comes into sight, a wave of recall hits me so fast it stuns me. Mom might be saying something, but I don't hear a word. Without seeing it, in an instant I remember the stairs just past the front door, the kitchen, the room I slept in, and the room Bailey slept in. I remember moving Bailey and myself into here when Kyle and I came home for Christmas and I made him leave us while he went back to Alberta. I remember a Christmas gathering. I remember lying on the floor and playing with Bailey. The job I found, the office I worked in, coffee dates with Sheri… and him.

The face that haunted me at Riverview, but I managed to forget about while I was so preoccupied with learning to live, comes back. With its vicious return, it's clear that there's no way I can live with myself if I don't confess to the love of my life what may or may not have been.

Thinking hard, even while I re-enter the home I know is home, the joy of my reunion with Bailey is tempered by the self-disgust I blissfully forgot about for a while. The comfort and security that flood over me are still rimmed with wrongness. The debauched feelings, the guilty conscience of not being emotionally faithful to the other half of my heart, detachment from my own heart and integrity… they're full-force once again.

Smiling on the outside, I wander through my safe haven and know that things here are just as they were before. This arouses my memory tenfold. So many things come back to me. I should feel absolutely euphoric. I'm overjoyed, but also desperate to know what exactly happened in those four months before the accident when I came back here from Alberta. My mind's eye doesn't reflect a huge window of time before the accident.

"Welcome home, babe."

I twitch hard at the interruption to my extremely porous and frustrating reflections. Looking up, my vision is filled with Kyle, my love, this solidly honourable man I have no choice but to hurt right now.

"Hey," I murmur. "How'd you get here so fast?"

I didn't have time to figure out how to tell him that I'm the last person to deserve him. There's no other choice. I have to tell him. This can't stay where it is, festering in my mind. It'll kill me.

But nothing might have happened! It might be absolutely nothing! What if I tell him and he leaves me, then years down the road it finally comes back to me and I realize that nothing happened?

My heart was in the wrong place. I can remember that much. Kyle has been such a rock; he has been here with me when I didn't know anyone or anything, when I looked like a rotting carcass and he had no way of knowing that I'd live; or if I did survive, if I'd ever have the mental capacity to love him back. How could I let him be ignorant of the thing about me that he'd walk away from if he knew?

My eyes strain to communicate this inward battle to Kyle without words. I don't want to have to say anything other than "Let's get married the moment I step out of Riverview."

"I left work," he says with a grin that could split his face. "I had to be here. I'm sorry I couldn't be the one to pick you up."

No way. Don't make this any harder than it is.

"Um," I say after clearing my throat several times. "Kyle, I have to tell you something. Can we go somewhere else? Outside?"

Kyle's brow furrows slightly, but he nods his head.

Yeah, you'll want to shake me out of your head.

"Yeah, sure, anything you want." The lightness in his voice isn't mirrored in his troubled face.

He helps me stand up and calls out to Mom that we'll be outside. The deafening silence I thought I left behind at Riverview falls around me again as I follow him out the backdoor onto the deck. He takes my hand to steady me as I step over the door's threshold, and I savour it. This is probably the last time he'll want to do any such thing.

In the same way I've done so many times at Riverview, my mind steps away from my body and escapes the present, even while my knowledge of the story pours of my mouth like acid. Once I start talking, I can't stop myself.

Kyle's face, though... is he hearing me? I'm telling him something that should make him get up and leave as fast as I got rammed by an eighty-thousand-pound truck, yet here he stands in front of me without dropping my sweating hand.

When I finally finish talking, because there's nothing left to say, I cast my eyes down and chew on my lip, waiting for the guillotine's blade to fall. He finally drops my hand to run both of his through his hair, but he still doesn't speak. My tension grows aggressively the longer he waits to say anything; very quickly, my spine spews razor blades into every surrounding nerve.

A warm hand covers mine again and makes me jump, punching even more pain into my neck. I hardly notice the sharp ache when I see that Kyle has picked up the hand he just dropped. He reaches for my other hand too. Stunned, I lift my eyes to his face; the humanitarian expression covering it is so confusing.

I don't understand.

"Amanda," he says, more softly than he has ever said anything. "I'm not sure what you all remember about before, but… well… we were in a pretty rocky place. It kind of sucks that this stuff might have happened, but the way things were with us, it didn't look like we had a sure future."

He moves my hand to look at the finger that would have worn my engagement ring.

"Your mom told me that she noticed you weren't wearing your ring about a month after I went back to Alberta. When you and I talked on the phone, less was said between us each time. After a while, we only called each other so Bailey could hear my voice."

His voice starts to catch. He's fighting tears that I don't think I've ever seen. At least, not while I've been sane enough to remember them.

"When I was transferred back home from Alberta, I moved into an apartment not too far from your parents' house. I wanted to pretend everything was great with us, and I wanted to be close to my little girl again." He sighs deeply, looking at my ring finger again. "Nothing was said about our upcoming wedding because it was already mostly planned anyway, but still, we didn't really talk about it. I'd hang out with Bailey all I could after work, and you were often there too, but we didn't connect the way we used to.

"Then, well… one evening you were going to hang out with Sheri, and then all of a sudden your mom showed up at my house and she was more freaked out than I've ever seen anyone." His tears are rolling now. "They never found your ring in the wreck, and I guess I didn't really expect them to. But Amanda, listen to me please."

He steps back, coughs, and clears his throat. The anger that should be on his face isn't there, though. I rub my eyes hard. What is going on?

"We both have our faults. We have both said and done some stupid things to each other. But Amanda," he steps closer, planting himself right in front of me, "that doesn't need to change anything." He pauses for a minute, then laughs weirdly. "Actually, a lot of things need to change. I mean, the way we are, with or without each other, needs to change. This whole insanity has shown me very clearly that us being together means everything to me, even though we both suck sometimes. But I can't stop loving you. Like, I stuck around through all of this, even though a lot of the time it didn't seem like there was any hope in staying because it looked like you weren't going to be okay.

"I was never really sure about God before. But it was so obvious that He was here; He showed me some real stuff in the sickest ways." Kyle laughs morbidly. "I needed something real to wake me up, and look what happened. I had no idea what was going on or what I was doing most of the time in the first month of this insanity, but I felt something telling me to stay in the weirdest way. And I wanted to. I didn't want to go anywhere but by your side. And then I saw miracles like I've never seen before. There was nothing to doubt. God was there the whole time."

Kyle's sombre face changes in the most beautiful way when we both hear a knock on the window behind me. He steps past me and opens the door, and Bailey comes toddling out.

"Dada!" she squeals, her chubby little arms uplifted. His face breaks into a smitten grin as he picks up his little girl and rubs his nose against hers. Her answering giggles lift my heart from where it lays at Kyle's feet. He moves Bailey to his hip and lifts her tiny hand up to rest it on my cheek. She doesn't pull back as she looks between us questioningly.

"Mommy," Kyle says. "This is mommy, Monkey."

Bailey's eyes keep darting between us before they rest on Kyle.

"Dada," she says, her tone not allowing for any kind of argument. I can't help but laugh; her stubbornness is suddenly as fresh in my memory as anything.

"She'll come around so fast, Amanda. No worries," Kyle reassures me urgently. "She's been asking for you so much. She's a toddler. She has no patience to sit still and be careful around you, but it'll be great soon. She knows you. She loves you."

It doesn't make sense to me how normal he's being. I just dropped a bomb on him, but he doesn't even seem to have heard me. I know he heard me, I know he responded to me, but now it's like nothing was said.

"Kyle." I don't know what to say. I said everything already.

He tugs cutely on Bailey's ear as he looks at me, as calm as ever. "Amanda, what's done is done. You told me. I really believe you would never do anything like that again, and besides," he looks heavenward and gives his head the tiniest shake, "I think we all understand what life means to us now. And what family means to us."

That's it. He sets his mouth in a way that says he's done talking about it. Dazed awe infiltrates me and I stand still, rooted to the spot. I did not just hear what I heard.

Did it sound like Kyle just forgave me completely for what I was so sure would be the ruin of our relationship? This man, who I now fully recall as being so unsure of God, just forgave me like Jesus.

As the evening passes into night and I'm snugly tucked into bed, the day's surreal events play through my head with all the effect of a big screen movie. Over and over again I watch the parts where I confess my villainy to Kyle, and he sets me free. I waver between disbelief and grateful shock.

Thank you, Jesus. Thank you, Jesus. Why do you keep on saving me like this? What have I done to deserve anything good from you?

The wages of sin is death, but the gift of God is eternal life in Christ Jesus our Lord.

This verse can only be divinely inspired. My God is speaking His gift into my soul.

The rest of the weekend passes more quickly than anything I can remember since waking up from my accident. My whole family is at my parents' house for the weekend: my brothers and their wives, my sister, aunts and uncles, and my precious friend Chelsea. I realize with delight, probably for the hundredth time, that Sheri is pregnant and I'm going to be an auntie.

The best thing, though, is that my precious Bailey is quickly becoming less distant. She even sits on my lap, with Kyle ready to dive in and grab her the second she looks like she might rattle my spine in any way. I kiss her head over and over again, revelling in this long-lost chance to smell her hair, feel her tiny warm body in my arms, and just be her mommy.

When Monday morning comes like a thief in the night, I keep hoping that the idea of returning to Riverview is just that—an idea.

Not so. Mom packs Bailey up for daycare and me for Riverview, and we pile into her car to head back to my jail cell. Mom promises over and over again while driving to Winnipeg that I'm almost done. Riverview will be a thing of the past before I know it, she keeps reassuring me.

When I walk back inside, the lights seem brighter. It doesn't immediately feel like a prison. The happy welcome-backs from everyone actually feel good. I finally understand deep in my heart that Riverview is a place of hope, not a place of despair. I feel ready to tackle this with everything I have.

Dr. Johnson intercepts me on my way to the lunchroom after the morning therapies, her usually professional face betraying the tiniest bit of eagerness.

"Amanda, hi!"

"Hey doc." I can't suppress my curious smile. "What's up?"

"Well, my dear, I had a good conversation with your mother about your weekend. I've also had some good conversations with your therapists and nurses, and reviewed your medical records." She lays a hand on my shoulder and looks me square in the face. "Amanda, you're going to be ready to go home at the end of this week."

"Another visit?" I can't believe I'm hearing this. "Yes! Thank you!"

It's hard not to jump up and down, but I can't stop myself from bouncing on my feet. The spinal sensation quickly puts an end to that.

"No, Amanda." Dr. Johnson says, trying and failing to subdue a laugh. "On Friday, you're going to go home. You are going to be discharged. You don't have to come back."

Awake

EVERY DAY OF THE PAST WEEK HAS BEEN THE LONGEST DAY IN HISTORY. Each therapy session has been more intense than the last; it's like they're prepping me for the military or something. The visits from people who mean the world to me have gotten sparser. Since I'm coming home at the end of the week, they'll see me soon anyway. Evenings in my room are broken up with short walks around Riverview's grounds, always escorted by Wade, Lori, or Anne. They're all so easy to talk to and I really enjoy the time they spend with me. But the moment they walk me back inside and up to my room, loneliness sets in.

But my last day is today, Wade says. I'm leaving here forever. I still have to eat breakfast and then to go down to physio for some final assessments, and I have to attend another meeting with Dr. Johnson. But after that, Mom is going to be here to take me home. I can't help but feel like I'll only believe it when I'm actually sitting in Mom's car again.

I watch every clock I can find as I go about the order of the morning's events as Wade laid them out. The clocks are almost moving backwards, and my anxiousness affects the way I interact with everyone.

"Girl, chill out," Wade barks at me before crumpling over in laughter. "You're so uptight! Amanda, you're going home today, and not only that, I see your mom and sister are here to pick you up. Don't get too crazy yet, though. You still need that meeting with Dr. Johnson."

My pulse quickens as I turn to see Mom and Vicki coming up behind me. I can actually feel the tension drop out of my face. They both break into a run and stop within a foot of me before leaning in for a gentle but fierce group hug. A mixture of sobs and relieved giggles burst out of our huddle, and Wade's booming laughter from behind the nurse's desk makes us crack up harder.

Eventually, Dr. Johnson breaks us up and ushers us into an office where we all sit, anxiously facing her.

"What a happy day," she says with that eager look on her face again. "I love this."

Mom, Vicki, and I just smile at her and each other.

"Okay, let's get started so you can go home, Amanda." She shuffles some papers around the desk and glances at a few of them. "You've had quite the go here, and you've got a ways to go yet once you go home, too. Besides the myofascial pain in your cervical spine, which you'll need to manage with continued physiotherapy, Ibuprofen, ice, and exercises, you'll need to also wear the CTO for car rides until a follow-up appointment with the spinal surgeon relieves you of that. Understand?"

"Yes," Mom and I both say, impatient to leave.

"As for your cognition, I see that you've got some moderate deficits in insight and judgement which will improve over the next year, but your short-term memory has improved substantially in the last two weeks." She glances at me over her glasses. "That will continue to improve as well. You've got some retrograde amnesia for about a year and a half prior to the accident, correct?"

I nod fractionally.

"That may or may not come back to you," she says. "It most likely won't."

"That's okay. I didn't die and I have my daughter." I pause in hesitation. Maybe the doctor won't share my view about Bailey's Guardian. It needs to be said, though. It needs to be sung from the rooftops. "God kept her safe and out of the vehicle when I smashed it, and that's amazing because she would have been with me if my mom hadn't changed her mind. It's okay; I can live without a few years."

Dr. Johnson just nods and smiles. "Your initial agitation and impulsive behaviour caused you to remove your CTO before it should have come off, and your left arm went slightly numb," she says, apparently unaffected by what I said. She reaches for my arm. "Has that corrected itself?"

"Yes, good as gold." Wow, I forgot that I did that until just now.

"We found you have an A/C joint separation—"

"A what?"

"A separated shoulder," she clarifies. "It was missed somehow in all the other injuries, but you have an appointment with an orthopaedic surgeon scheduled in two weeks. You have diplopia when you look to the right, correct?"

"What?" She's got to stop using these big words. I can't wait to go home and not hear all this medical terminology anymore.

"Double vision," she says patiently.

"Oh yeah."

"That may improve slightly over the next few months, but it's highly doubtful that it'll return to normal."

"Like I said before, that's fine."

There's no need to go over all this. I just want to go home to my baby and my family. Dr. Johnson sees me eye the clock on the wall behind her. She chuckles and runs through the rest of her spiel more quickly.

Finally, armed with a few prescriptions and pages of notes, we emerge from Dr. Johnson's office. As we return to my room to get my stuff, the feeling only gets more dreamlike.

Lori and Anne intercept us at the door with flowers and a farewell card. The well wishes of these two mean more to me than they might ever know. Some days they were the only ones giving me any sort of hope or drive to keep going. I hug them both too vigorously and feel it in all the wrong places, but I don't care. I love them, and who knows if and when I'll see them again.

When we reach the desk to sign the discharge papers, Wade saunters around to the side we stand on. With his hands on his hips, he grins like an idiot, shaking his head at me.

"Well, well, look at you, getting up out of here," he crows. "It's been a long haul, girl, but you deserve it."

"Thanks Wade," I say through the tears I feel brewing behind my eyes. "Wade..."

I don't know what to say to this nurse who has been like a brother to me. I need to say something, though. He needs to know how much he has meant to me.

I can't form a single word. They all just run down my cheeks. I smile stupidly at Wade and shrug. His always light-hearted, good-natured face breaks into a genuine beam as he opens his arms. I move forward and hug him just like I hugged the girls, too enthusiastically for my neck. It doesn't matter. He needs to know how important he's been, just like other two.

The most confusing feelings enfold me as Mom, Vicki, and I walk out of the place that I had no idea even existed until it contained my entire existence. I hated it here, yet leaving it behind is bittersweet. I learned humanity again here, maybe even for the first time.

I feel like I can't ask for anything else. A completely undeserved amount of grace has fallen on me. In all the knowledge I have of my life before, there wasn't a thing about me that could have been worthy of grace.

As far as I can remember, I wasn't in the right place before I came here. Never mind the drugs, alcohol, love in all the wrong places, or anything else; that was all empty enough, but the biggest void was in my soul. I had no room for God in the scattered pieces of my life.

A bird chirps brightly in the tree branches over Mom's car, and it sounds like it's singing right at me. Vicki follows my gaze, and when she sees the bird, she smiles and pecks me on the cheek.

"I can't wait for you to see the world again."

The joy inscribed in every feature of her face sparks even more hope in me. I remember now, for the first time, that Vicki and I haven't been close in a long time. That's not okay. She's my sister.

"Vicki." I pull her close and hold her as tight as my brittle frame lets me.

"Aw, what?" She pulls her face back from where my crushing hug forced it and looks at me inquisitively.

"I love you. I hope you know that."

Vicki ducks back into the hug again before I can see her face.

"I know," she whispers into my shoulder. "I love you."

Driving through Winnipeg for the second time in my new reality, the commonness of it is again completely new and brilliant. My Creator, the Creator of everything there ever was and will be, has given me new life to walk out into all of this one more time. He is here, going before and behind me. I am on holy ground. I can't miss this second chance to be His servant.

For me to live is Christ and to die is gain.

My soul smiles at its Lover, who has taken me, His wayward child, and called me to His side with all the compassion of the Father that He is.

Coming back to the real world with a new commission written all over my heart has me shivering in the summer heat flowing through my open car window. It took me dying to my old self to truly find myself, and the undecorated understanding of what I need to do now sends chills up and down my rehabilitated backbone. The God of the universe is everywhere. He is waiting for everyone to open their eyes and see Him.

> *"You are my witnesses,"* declares the Lord, *"and my servant whom I have chosen, so that you may know and believe me…"*
> —Isaiah 43:10

I will never get used to the Scriptures spoken to the depths of my core at the exact right times. My Father is walking with me and talking to me—not in words I can hear, but His Word, which resonates so deeply. The thing for me to do now is declare the love and mercy He freely gave me when I was so far from deserving it.

In my wake, I've been called to walk alongside people and steer them in the direction of restoration to Christ, in the same way I have been restored to life by the angels God sent me.

Afterword

The rest of the story: Amanda walked down the aisle as a beautiful bride six months after the accident (Kyle was one of the few grooms who understood what the words "for better or worse" meant, as there was still a long road of recovery ahead). Amanda and Kyle were then publically baptized, declaring their Jesus relationship, and Amanda later gave birth to a beautiful baby boy. Three years later, she ran a half-marathon for the glory of the Father.

—Pastor Glen Siemens